RESCUE

True Stories of the U.S. Life-Saving Service

Edited by John J. Galluzzo
Foreword By Frederick Stonehouse

Avery Color Studios, Inc.
Gwinn, Michigan

United States Life-Saving Service Heritage Association
Hull, Massachusetts

ISBN: 978-1-892384-59-1

Library of Congress Control Number: 2011901144

First Edition–2011

10 9 8 7 6 5 4 3 2 1

Published by Avery Color Studios, Inc.
Gwinn, Michigan 49841

Association Information:

The United States Life-Saving Service Heritage Association

P.O. Box 213

Hull, Massachusetts 02045

www.uslife-savingservice.org

www.facebook.com/uslssh

www.twitter.com/uslssha

Table Of Contents

FOREWORD

by Frederick Stonehouse

The popular press called them, "Storm Warriors" and "Heroes of the Surf." And they were always good copy in magazines and newspapers of the period. Books aimed at youngsters used the theme of, "Adventure at the Life-Saving Station." In 1925 Paramount even produced a feature film, "Rugged Water" starring Wallace Beery among other period stars. Parker Brothers also produced a board game, "The Life-Saving Game," kind of a spin off from "Chutes and Ladders." Millions of people saw demonstration Life-Saving Service crews trained by the legendary Keeper Henry J. Cleary of Marquette (Michigan, Lake Superior) perform the breeches buoy, surf and lifeboat drills at the great national expositions and fairs. World famous figures like the famous Apache Indian war chief Geronimo and President William McKinley made a point of seeking them out at the events. Geronimo became a favorite of the Life-Saving Service crew often taking rides in the boats with many of his entourage. Buffalo Bill's Wild West Show even featured Life-Saving demonstrations to the cheers of huge crowds.

The common thread was the recognition of the powerful story of the U.S. Life-Saving Service and it's potent impact on American culture.

What makes the story so remarkable, especially in the current age of "factoid" journalism, was with the exception of the novels and film (which it can be argued at least were based in part on true events), the material published about the exploits of the Life-Saving Service was true. The surfmen regularly performed desperate rescues against overwhelming odds, were paid a mere pittance and were loyal and courageous. Although merely mortals, they were often seen as near superhuman.

When the Life-Saving Service and Revenue-Marine were merged in January 1915 to form the new U.S. Coast Guard many of the old traditions of daring do, fighting against all odds to make the rescue remained. After all it was largely the same men under a different name. As the decades passed new equipment was fielded including big motor lifeboats and large steam powered cutters. Then it was diesel that drove boats big and small. Aluminum winged monsters cut the air above, vastly increasing capability. Seamen who could drive a boat through a crashing surf and row for hours to make a rescue, pound miles over the grasping sand of a desolate beach in the teeth of a nor'easter looking for shipwreck victims, or man lonely lookout towers high above wave whipped seas to find vessels in distress became obsolete.

It was a new age when technology slowly but inexorably emerged on the rescue scene. Some thought it would supplant man; the machine was the important part not the human! The reality was much different. It was the man who drove the machine, not the reverse. And when the machine failed, it was the man who found another way to accomplish the mission.

For those of us who study history we know the more things change the more they are the same. It is still a case of the man (or in today's Coast Guard just as likely to be a woman) in the boat. These descendents of the old Life-Savers are the ultimate weapon whether fighting crashing seas and screaming winds to rescue a lost boater or intercepting enemies of humanity be they drug smugglers or terrorists. The old traditions of the Life-Saving Service continue!

Introduction

by John J. Galluzzo

Since the United States Life-Saving Service Heritage Association put out its first volume of collected stories from the pages of *Wreck & Rescue Journal*, the organization has completed a national inventory of the extant buildings of the Life-Saving Service. Our fears were confirmed; less than half of the original buildings remain.

Of those that remain, several are in dire circumstances. Vermilion, Michigan, is ready to fall over, after years of sheer abandonment. The stations in Long Branch, New Jersey, a collection of three, outstanding architectural specimens, seem doomed to bow in the face of shoreline development. Ocean City, New Jersey, also has a developer's target on it. Kittery, Maine's Wood Island station has outlived its time in place. When it was built at the mouth of Portsmouth Harbor, it was a lone sentinel, a welcome sight for mariners heading in and out of the Piscataqua River. Now, it's desolate and unused, too far from the mainland for any feasible purposes, as far as the community knows.

That's why our organization is more important than ever.

Whether these buildings remain standing or not in future years, their stories must be told, tales of shipwreck and rescue, of standing watch against the enemy of the day, of vigilance, of heroism. *Wreck & Rescue Journal* has now been their forum for fifteen years, but the storytelling has just begun.

In the pages that follow, you'll be introduced to Middle Island, Michigan, and Manomet, Massachusetts, to Cape Lookout, North Carolina, and Oregon's Point Adams. There'll be lifeboats and surfmen, cries of "Ship Ashore!" with life and death walking a line together. But the truth is that only a tiny fraction of the greater tale is being told.

What was the greatest rescue attempt ever to be undertaken by the crew of the Crumple Island station in Maine? Did the Brazos, Texas, crew ever mutiny? Was the Nome, Alaska, station known for its rugged, old salt keeper, or was that more of a Lorain, Ohio, thing? While the country's top historians have been researching and writing about the history of the Life-Saving Service and the early Coast Guard for generations, most of the story is still uncovered.

In the meantime, *Wreck & Rescue Journal* rolls on in step with the activities of the members of USLSSHA. Annual meeting destinations continue to inspire new members to come aboard. In 2009, the crew visited the stations from Lewes, Delaware, to Assateague, Virginia. In 2010, the focus will shift northward to Spring Lake, New Jersey, and in 2011, the organization will return to Astoria, Oregon, for an exploration of the Coast Guard history of the Pacific Northwest.

History is there for the taking, for the pondering and for the interpreting. We hope that you will join us in expanding this national knowledge database by telling us what is important about your hometown life-saving station and contributing to *Wreck & Rescue Journal*, and helping to keep the architecture, artifacts and stories of the life-savers of old alive.

SECTION I:
Honor, Respect And Devotion To Duty

THE PENDLETON RESCUE

by Captain W. Russell Webster, USCG
(Volume 5, Issue 3)

It has been fifty years since First Class Boatswain's Mate (BM1) Bernard Webber and his volunteer crew of three took their 36-foot wooden motorized lifeboat out over the Chatham, Massachusetts, bar in 60-foot seas and 70-knot winds and rescued thirty-two men from the stricken tank vessel *Pendleton*.[1] Despite the passage of time, memories - especially the death of a thirty-third crewman during the rescue - still are vivid for the 73-year old small boat coxswain.

This is a story of unparalleled heroism by a Coast Guard small boat crew.

The *Pendleton's* Voyage

The 503-foot, 10,448 gross ton tank vessel *Pendleton* (T2-SE-A1 or "T2") departed Baton Rouge on 12 February with a full cargo of Kerosene and heating oil and a crew of forty-one, including the master, captain John Fitzgerald. Late on 17 February, the ship arrived off Boston. The weather was foul with extremely limited visibility, and the captain opted to stand off and headed his vessel at slow speed into Massachusetts Bay. Wind and sea conditions worsened throughout the night, building into a full-scale Nor'easter gale with snow and high seas.

By 0400 on 18 February, the *Pendleton* was shipping seas over her stern but appeared to be riding well. Sometime after, she rounded the tip of Cape Cod off Provincetown and assumed a more southerly course.

At about 0550, after a series of explosive cracking noises, the *Pendleton* took a heavy lurch and broke in two. Gone with the darkened

Jacobs ladder dangling over her side, the stern of the SS Pendleton *sits forlornly on a sand bar off the coast of Cape Cod. Coast Guardsmen from the Chatham Lifeboat Station overcame mountainous seas to rescue the survivors from this section of the vessel. The survivors climbed down the Jacobs ladder and then dropped into the rescue boat. Official USCG Photo*

bow section were the captain and seven crewmen, all destined to perish. In the stern, which continued to operate normally, including all machinery and lighting, Chief Engineer Raymond Sybert took charge and mustered his thirty-two survivors.

In mountainous seas, the stern section and its human cargo drifted south, with a slight port list, about six miles off Cape Cod. The bow also drifted south, but farther offshore. No SOS had been issued.[2]

Two Tankers in Trouble

On 18 February 1952, the Coast Guard would rescue seventy men from the seas. Like the *Pendleton*, the T2 tank vessel *Fort Mercer* had also split in half off Cape Cod, about twenty miles offshore.

The first news to reach the Chatham Lifeboat Station was regarding the *Fort Mercer*. With orders to launch a motorized lifeboat (MLB) to assist the tanker, the station officer in charge, Boatswain Cluff, ordered Chief Boatswain's Mate Donald Bangs to select his crew and man the *CG36383* at Stage Harbor. At the time, BM1 Webber thought, "My God, do they really think a lifeboat can make it that far out in this storm and find a ship amid blinding snow and raging seas with only a compass to guide it? If the crew doesn't freeze to death first, how will they get the men off the storm-tossed sections of the broken tanker?"[3]

On the stern of the *Pendleton*, Sybert's crew sighted the beach at about 1400. At 1455, the Chatham Lifeboat Station's radar picked up two blips about five and a half miles distant. At 1500, Bos'n Cluff visually sighted the bow section of the *Pendleton* and reported the contact to the Boston regional Coast Guard headquarters; Coast Guard PBY aircraft No. 1242 was diverted from ongoing rescue operations involving the *Fort Mercer* and shortly after 1600 made the first positive identification of both sections of the *Pendleton*. The Coast Guard now knew it had two stricken tankers and four possible rescue situations.[4]

Bos'n Cluff's initial reaction was to dispatch his remaining crew, including BM1 Webber, to North Beach in hopes they could render assistance to the *Pendleton's* crew if either section of the vessel came ashore. It soon became apparent that neither section would come ashore there, however, and the crew returned to the station to prepare the *CG36500* MLB to render aid.

Bos'n Cluff ordered Webber to "pick yourself a crew. Y'all got to take the 36500 out over the bar and assist that ship, ya-heah?" With great trepidation, knowing his likely fate but understanding his duty, he replied, "Yes, sir. I'll get ready."[5]

Only three men were available, as "other crew members had made themselves scarce when they heard *CG36500* was to be sent," but all quickly volunteered.[6] Webber was joined by the station's junior engineer, Engineman Andrew Fitzgerald, Seaman Richard Livesly, and Seaman Irving Maske, a crewman from the nearby Stonehorse Light Ship who had been waiting for transportation back.

At about 1730, as BM1 Webber and his crew readied their dory to row out to the *CG36500*, local fisherman and neighbor John Stello yelled out, "You guys better get lost before you get too far out."[7] Webber knew what his friend was suggesting: go out and probably die or get "lost" and live to talk about it.

Proceed as Directed

At 1755, Webber and his crew left the pier in their wooden 36-foot motorized lifeboat, driven by its single 90-horsepower gas engine. Turning into the channel, Webber could see the station's lights and hoped for a recall. Hearing nothing, he radioed the station and received the curt response, "Proceed as directed."[8]

As they approached Chatham's bar, the small-boat crew began to sing "Rock of Ages" and "Harbor Lights," but their voices were drowned out by the roar of the ocean colliding with the sand bar.[9] Crossing over, the *CG36500* was smashed by a wave and thrown high in the air, landing on her side. The self-righting boat recovered quickly and was smite again; this time tons of seawater crashed over the boat, breaking its windshield and flattening Webber.

Scrambling to his feet, Webber noticed the boat's compass had been knocked off its mount. The cold, near-hurricane-force winds howled through the cockpit as he struggled to regain control and steer in to the towering waves.

On the *Pendleton*, the engineer and his crew sensed their demise as the stern hulk hobby-horsed southward, smashing bottom with each new wave. Although several Coast Guard cutters and the *CG36383* were nearby, only the *CG36500* and her crew would be given one attempt to save Sybert and his men.

When Webber finally got the *CG36500* across the bar, he knew the water was deeper because the space between waves had increased, as had the wave heights.[10] Weather observations from nearby cutters indicated sea heights of forty to sixty feet.[11]

Occasionally, when the waves rolled the vessel over, the gasoline engine would lose its prime and die out. Each time, Engineer Fitzgerald crawled into the cramped compartment to restart it, and each time he was rewarded with severe burns, bruises, but finally the steady chug-chug of the engine and the relief and appreciation of his shipmates.

The boat proceeded roller coaster fashion, laboring up one side of a huge wave and surfing down the back side. Coxswain Webber knew too much speed was not good and, unchecked, would cause the bow to bury in the next wave and swamp the small vessel.[12] He had to reverse the engine on the back side of each wave to slow the boat down.

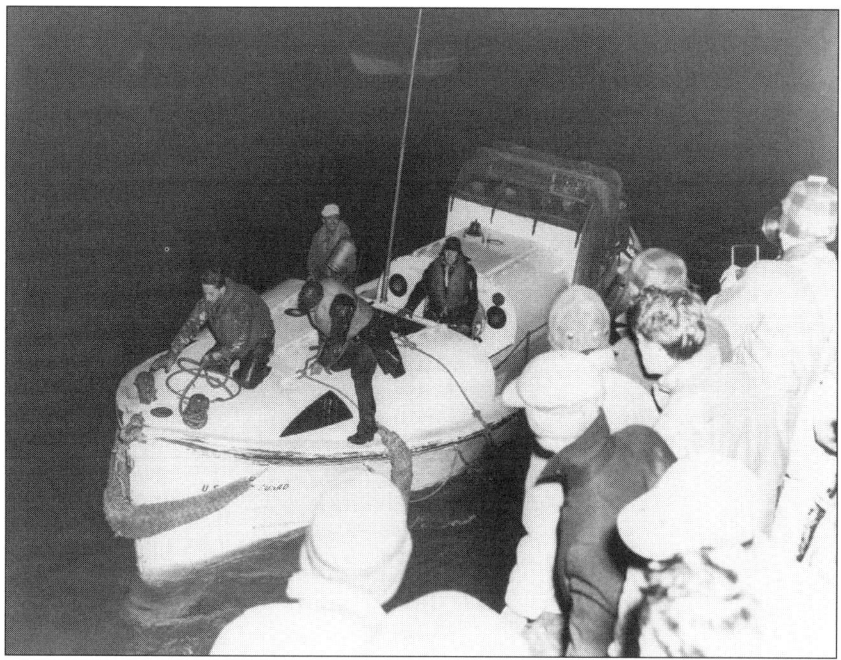

The rescue boat CG36500 *returned to the Chatham Fish Pier with 32 survivors of the tanker* Pendleton *after the rescue at sea. EN3 Andrew Fitzgerald was on the bow ready to handle the tie up at the pier. The other three men were* Pendleton *survivors. Photo by Richard C. Kelsey, Chatham, Mass. Photo credit: Cape Cod Community College.*

The first navigational waypoint was the Pollock Rip Light Ship, where Webber hoped to reorient himself and give his crew a breather in the lee of the larger vessel. Weather and visibility had worsened, and freezing horizontal snow lashed the coxswain's face through the broken windshield. He wore no lifejacket to give himself the best chance to react and guide the vessel. After about an hour of struggling, fearing he had missed the lightship, Webber slowed the *CG36500* to a near standstill as he sensed, rather than saw, something ahead. He sent a crewman forward to energize the boat's small searchlight. Within seconds, the light was on, but a large wave lifted the crewman up and over the coxswain flat and carried him aft, where he landed with a thud, but miraculously unhurt.

Webber crept the boat forward, and the searchlight soon revealed a black mass of twisted metal, which heaved high in the air on the massive waves then settled back in a "frothing mass of foam".[13] Each move produced a cacophony of groans as the broken ship strained in the 60-foot seas. No lights were apparent as Webber maneuvered the small boat aft along the port side of the *Pendleton's* stern section.

Leaping to Safety

Rounding the stern, the *CG36500's* searchlight illuminated the word *Pendleton*, and moments later, the larger vessel's own deck lights became apparent. A small figure above began waving his arms frantically, then disappeared.

Quickly, people began to line the *Pendleton's* starboard stern area, many shouting instructions, which were unintelligible over the wind and crashing seas. Webber looked on their position as "inviting" relative to his own and was considering strategies for how he and his crew could join them when a Jacob's ladder was tossed over the side and, unbelievably, men started down like a procession of ants.[14] The first man was dunked in the water like a tea bag then lifted fifty feet in the air as the *Pendleton* rolled and heaved. Webber sent his crew forward to assist as he maneuvered the *CG36500* along the *Pendleton's* starboard quarter. One by one, the tanker's survivors jumped, crashing on the tiny boat's bow or falling into the sea, where crewmen were sling-shotted out from the ship on the Jacob's ladder by the whipping of the waves. As they had reached their zenith of flight, the ship would snap them back and slam them against the hulk.

After multiple approaches and twenty men recovered, the *CG36500* began to handle sluggishly, but the human parade continued to descend. There was no turning back, and Webber decided they all would live or they all would die.[15]

And so it went as Webber and his crew literally stuffed their rescuees into the boat and risked life and limb again and again. Finally, with thirty-two survivors recovered, there remained at the bottom of the ladder only George "Tiny" Myers, a 300-pound giant of a man and the inspiration of the *Pendleton* crew for his personal heroics. Myers had distinguished himself by helping his thirty-two shipmates before considering his own situation.

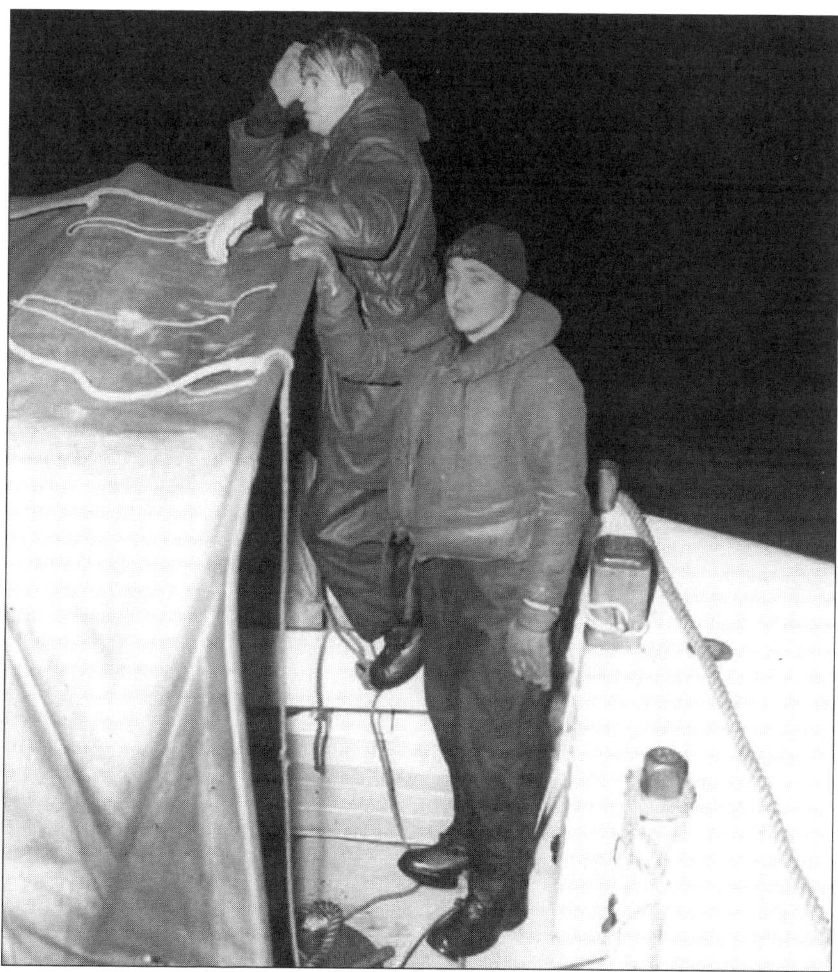

Seaman Irving Maske (foreground) and BM1 Bernard Webber in the coxswain's flat [on] board the CG36500 *following the dramatic rescue of 32 men off the stern of the* Pendleton *on Feb. 18, 1952. Photo by Richard C. Kelsey, Chatham, Mass. Photo credit: Cape Cod Community College.*

Myers jumped too soon and was swallowed up by the sea. Moments later, he was visible underneath the stern, clinging to one of the *Pendleton's* 11-foot propeller blades.

Easing ahead cautiously, Webber felt the stern of his small boat rise as a monstrous wave overtook her. The *CG36500* was driven ahead faster and faster toward Myers. Webber backed his engine hard, but the boat smashed into the *Pendleton* and Tiny Myers. The *CG36500* was ejected from underneath the *Pendleton* by another large wave just as the hulk was lifted one last time and rolled over again and sank.

All was again dark as the *CG36500's* searchlight was extinguished. Coxswain Webber was sickened at losing Tiny, but he knew the fate of the thirty-six men on his small boat still rested in his hands.[16]

Coming Home

With no compass and zero visibility, Webber had just two choices: head east into the seas and hope to survive ten to twelve hours until daylight brought the slim chance of transferring passengers to a larger rescue ship; or put the wind and seas on the small boat's stern and let them force the vessel ashore someplace where help might be nearby.

Webber tried his radio again and received an immediate acknowledgment. Once he briefed his superior that he had thirty-two *Pendleton* survivors on board, a squabble ensued between the nearby cutter

The Gold Medal crew relaxed at the station with coffee and doughnuts after a wild night at sea. Left to right: BM1 Bernard Webber, EN3 Andrew Fitzgerald, SN Richard Livesey and SN Irving Maske. Photo by Richard C. Kelsey, Chatham, Mass. Photo credit: Cape Cod Community College.

McCulloch and the Chatham station about options - including an at-sea rendezvous with the *McCulloch* and a second transfer of survivors.[17]

Webber turned off the radio and devised his own plan to beach the *CG36500* at the first opportunity.[18] The small vessel would be held on the beach as long as possible with the engine while the survivors clamored ashore. The *Pendleton* crew gave a cheer of approval and support and on they went. Very soon, a flashing red light appeared, and incredibly, the boat's searchlight revealed the buoy marking the turn to Old Harbor, Chatham, and safe water. A quick call to the station was met with excitement, for everyone knew that the rescued were now survivors. After another stream of overdirection and gibberish, Webber once again secured the radio after requesting assistance at the fish pier.

A crowd of men, women and children met the *CG36500*, securing lines and helping the shocked and, in some cases, sobbing survivors and rescuers ashore.[19]

In a message to the Chatham Lifeboat Station the day after the rescue, Rear Admiral H. G. Bradbury, Commander of the First Coast Guard District, sent his personal congratulations to BM1 Webber and his crew for their "Outstanding seamanship and utter disregard of your own safety in crossing the hazardous waters of Chatham bar in mountainous seas, extreme darkness, and falling snow during a violent gale to rescue from imminent death thirty-two crewmembers...minutes before the tanker capsized."[20] Webber and his three crewmembers all received the Treasury Department's Gold Lifesaving Medal for "Extreme and heroic daring" during the *Pendleton* rescue.[21]

SECTION II:
Beginnings

A Rich Family History: Captain Benjamin Rich and the Mass Humane Society

by John J. Galluzzo
(Volume 7, Issue 4)

Born on December 12, 1775 in Truro, Benjamin Rich headed out to sea as a cabin boy at thirteen years of age, to take part in the Canton trade, making four major voyages over the next six years. In 1794, at age 19, he made his first voyage to the Far East as a ship's master, a calling he would follow for the next six years.

Like all overseas merchants of the time, the young man faced a variety of dangers while heading from port to port. In 1798 the fledgling United States entered into the Quasi-War with France without a national navy, leaving its merchant seamen virtually unprotected. Pirates still roamed the high seas in search of plunder, especially the supposedly easily-attainable goods to be pulled from vessels returning from the Far East with furniture, rugs, clothing and spices.

Rich's most intense encounter took place off of Algiers. There, "he was attacked...by two French privateers both of which, with his characteristic intrepidity, he fought a whole summer's day; and at last, when his shot was all expended and he had charged his cannon with whatever he could find on board, he succeeded in beating them off" (Reverend Alexander D. D. Young, quoted in Julia Rich Hogan's "A Rich to Remember," The Rich Family Association Kinfolk, June, 1970, p. 11).

On March 31, 1800, at age 24, Benjamin Rich married Susanna Heath of Roxbury, a change in lifestyle that pulled him away from the helm of his ships. In 1801, he retired from the sea and began a new phase of his life, as one of the leading commerce experts in Boston. He had prepared himself "by personal observations of various parts of the world and large intercourse with the inhabitants of other climes and intimate acquaintance with the products of foreign lands" (Young, in Hogan, p. 12).

At that time he also began a family. In 1802, Susanna gave birth to their first child, Benjamin, Jr., who grew up to join his father in the family business, Benjamin Rich and son, but sadly died an early death by consumption in the West Indies in 1829. A second child, daughter Susanna, died the year following her birth, while a second son, Samuel Heath Rich, known by the epithet "Gentleman Sam, tall and fine," died in 1846 in Calcutta, by one account, or in Hong Kong, by another. Son Charles became a Congregational minister in Springfield, Illinois, described by Shebnah Rich in his 1883 Truro, Cape Cod, or Land Marks and Sea Marks as "a cultivated Christian gentleman, social and genial" (p. 389). As for the rest of the family line, the story remains clouded. Hogan states that "two daughters, Susan and Elizabeth, survived the smallpox epidemic in Boston and later married," (p.12), while Shebnah Rich tells the story of two gravesites "upon the steep hill top, northwest of Ebenezer Freeman's house, in a little enclosure" where "are buried two members of (Benjamin Rich's) family who died in Boston of small-pox." (p. 389). One other daughter did survive to marry the successful Mr. Larkin of the firm of Larkin and Stackpole.

In 1811, Rich embarked on a career in philanthropy, that year being chosen as a trustee of the young Humane Society of the Commonwealth of Massachusetts, an organization dedicated to the "recovery of persons, who meet with such accidents as produce in them the appearance of death, and for promoting the cause of humanity, by pursuing such means, from time to time, as shall have for their object the preservation of human life, and the alleviation of its miseries" ("Rules and By-Laws of the Massachusetts Humane Society," quoted in Mark Anthony DeWolfe Howe's History of the Humane Society of the Commonwealth of Massachusetts, 1918, p. 269). His association with the society would last for 33 years.

Perhaps Rich's heartfelt dedication to the Society's causes stemmed from the loss of his younger brother Nehemiah at sea in 1804. Or perhaps a deeper, inherent sense of bravery and nobility of spirit drew him to that organization. In May of 1818 Rich displayed his own personal courage following an explosion aboard a Canton packet tied up in Boston Harbor. Focusing solely on the fact that lives were in danger, the 42-year old leapt onto the deck through the dancing flames, disregarding the possibility of secondary explosions, and rescued the crew.

While serving in his 19th year as a trustee in 1829, Rich had the distinction of being elected as the Ninth President of the Massachusetts Humane Society, a position he would hold until 1843. During his tenure he had the privilege of launching the Society into what historian Mark Anthony DeWolfe Howe describes as the "golden age" of the society, from 1840 until the successful restructuring of the federal United States Life-Saving Service by Sumner Kimball in 1871.

The Society had built the first American lifeboat on Nantucket in 1807, placing it in Cohasset that year. The boat remained there until 1813, but succeeding that date no records of lifeboats along the Massachusetts coast exist until 1840. Although the society had successfully maintained a series of houses of refuge along the coast since 1787, in January of that year, Rich and the board of trustees expressed their desire to re-enter the world of organized shore-based lifesaving of mariners in distress at sea, in the wake of the triple hurricanes of December 1839, but found that the coffers of the Society would not yield sufficient funds to construct any new boats.

In April, the state legislature sent a communication to the surprised board, a resolve passed on March 21, providing, "That there be allowed and paid out of the Treasury of the Commonwealth, to the President and Trustees of the Massachusetts Humane Society, the sum of five thousand dollars, for the purpose of furnishing Life Boats to be stationed at the most exposed parts of the seacoast within this Commonwealth..." In a letter dated January 4, 1841, the Society informed the legislature that eleven boats had been constructed and placed appropriately from Plum Island to Martha's Vineyard.

The following year the state approved a $1350 grant to the Humane Society for the same purpose, allowing them to construct and place more boats. In his report to the legislature in January of 1842, Rich told the story of the success of the lifeboats by alluding to the rescue of 28 lives, but also warned governmental leaders of the importance of maintaining a rigid schedule of boat repair. "In the gale of the 17th of December last, when the ship Mohawk was cast on shore at Nantasket Beach, when the life boat stationed there was launched into the surf, and, in endeavoring to save the crew, she was driven on the rocks and badly stove. Since which she has been brought to the city and is now repairing, will be finished soon and re-placed in its proper station, the cost of which will be from sixty to eighty dollars. These boats will be constantly wanting repairs, painting etc. etc., and it will be necessary that a small appropriation should be made for that purpose..." (Benjamin Rich to John Davis, January 11, 1842). The wreck of the Mohawk represented future Point Allerton Life-Saving Station keeper Joshua James' first recorded rescue, at age 15.

In 1845, 18 Society lifeboats guarded the Massachusetts coast; by 1876, that number had grown to 60.

But Rich, now entering his late sixties, felt that the time had arrived to allow a younger man to take the role as the society's leader, for he as well had other goals in life he hoped to achieve. A highly religious man, he had already raised the necessary funds to preserve his church's spire, when the need arose for a new fence around the building. Through his efforts, that fence soon stood.

In October, 1841, after a devastating storm claimed the lives of 60 fishermen from his native Truro, he walked the streets of Boston tirelessly, conscripting almost $6,000 for the relief of the 27 widows and 51 children of the lost men. In all, the population of Barnstable County included more than 900 widows of the sea by 1841.

Responding to his letter of resignation on 1844, the trustees of the Society expressed their appreciation for his devoted decades of service. "You have been instrumental in providing for the wants and relief of the needy and shipwrecked mariners. You have superintended the building and the localities of our life-boats. To yourself...belong(s) emphatically the praise of this grand scheme of relief to the brave mariner in the hour of dreadful peril. Enjoy the high estimate you hold in this community, as a merchant and a philanthropist. Accept our best wishes for your future happiness and usefulness; and when your sun sets, may it be in the serenity of a green old age" (Quoted in S. Rich, p. 389).

The Rich family continued his tradition of involvement with coastal lifesaving. Captain Mulford Rich of Wellfleet boarded 25 wrecks and saved 29 lives over the course of his life, earning a Society gold medal for the rescue of the crew of the Franklin in 1849. Captain Benjamin

Swett Rich served as superintendent of the U.S.L.S.S.'s Fifth Life-Saving District, along the coasts of Delaware and Virginia, from 1875 until his death in 1900. Anthony Atwood Rich contracted and built the Cahoon's Hollow Life-Saving Service Station in Wellfleet in 1885.

On June 3, 1851, Benjamin Rich died at his Boston home at 75 years, 5 months, and 22 days old. The next morning all of the ships in Boston Harbor dropped their flags to half-mast in his honor.

New York Roots: The Life Saving Benevolent Association

by Van R. Field
(Volume 6, Issue 2)

The Humane Society of the Commonwealth of Massachusetts was the first organization to attempt to save mariners wrecked on the shores of the new United States. They built the first house of refuge for shipwrecked sailors on the beach at Lovell's Island in Boston Harbor in 1787. The organization of volunteers continued building such huts, equipped with stoves, firewood and some food and clothing, into the nineteenth century. Eventually they branched out into larger buildings equipped with surfboats and rescue equipment. The stations had paid captains, the overseers of the equipment and the leaders of small crews who would arrive to work a shipwreck. They were paid a small amount for their services when needed. The Humane Society continued their rescue work into the 1930s.

A few hundred miles to the south, immigrants from Europe arrived in New York in ever increasing numbers through the 1830s and 40s. In 1838 alone, more than 25,000 immigrants arrived. By 1849 almost 222,000 had come ashore. Immigrants usually arrived in old sailing ships in poor condition and often in winter when passage rates were low. Only the rich could afford transport on the new steamships.

By 1900 this tide of immigrants, mostly from Ireland, where the potato famine had hit hard, had peaked. Most of the shipwrecks along the northeastern shore were cargo ships with small crews.

William A. Newell, a physician who was later elected to the House of Representatives, was on the beach in New Jersey attending a patient when a winter storm struck the coast. During the storm, Newell had the unfortunate opportunity to witness firsthand the wreck of the Austrian brig *Terasto* and the death of thirteen of its crew. The ship had stranded on the bar, beyond the reach and capability of the local fishermen to render any assistance. They were unable to launch their dory into the raging sea.

At the time of the loss of the *Terasto*, the federal government was gradually easing into the business of safety for ships doing business in American ports. In 1789 they passed a bill to establish federal lighthouses, Boston Light being first, followed by others including New Jersey's Montauk Point. In 1806 a Coast survey was undertaken to make navigational charts. In 1838 steamboat inspection was inaugurated.

In 1847 Dr. Newell managed to attach some funds to a lighthouse bill for coastal lifesaving equipment. The next year more funds were appropriated and construction was begun on equipment garages on the beach. The first house was built near Sandy Hook, N.J. in Spermaceti Cove.

In 1849 stations were built on both the New Jersey and Long Island, New York, coastlines. The Secretary of the Treasury's Revenue Marine was put in the position of overseeing the operation including equipping these buildings.

Captain Douglas Ottinger of the Revenue Marine accepted this challenge. He formed a loose committee to do the job, consisting of the Board of Underwriters, wreckmasters and surfmen. He worked with Joseph Francis, a lifeboat builder in Brooklyn, NY, who was then building corrugated, galvanized iron boats with air chambers and cork fenders for use on ships. These boats were furnished along with other rescue equipment and were stored in the buildings on the beach. The buildings were locked up and the keys left with nearby responsible fishermen, or others who could raise volunteer crews.

Captain Ottinger ran tests on line-carrying rockets and a small "eprouvette" mortar that had been developed in England years earlier by a Captain Manby, an artillery officer. The mortar shot a ball with a line attached with great success.

Francis worked on a small metal life-car that could ride on a line out to a ship and back, carrying the shipwrecked persons.

The system got its first big test when on January 12, 1850, the British ship Ayrshire, carrying immigrants to New York, stranded in a snowstorm. Wreckmaster John Maxon and his volunteer crew from Squan Beach, New Jersey, shot a line over the ship and using the new Francis life-car brought 201 of the 202 people on the ship ashore safely. One person refused to get into the crowded, enclosed life-car and tried to sit on the outside. He was swept away and lost.

The following is an excerpt from a letter written to Congress concerning the wreck, an attempt to justify the expenditure of more money on lifesaving equipment, penned by Walter R. Jones, President of the Life Saving Benevolent Association:

> "Next was an emigrant ship called the AYRSHIRE with 169 passengers [and 33 crew] stranded in a snow storm on Squan Beach on the shore of N.J., on the 13th of last month. The gale was so violent that no boat could approach or leave the ship. The carronade provided by the Government brought to the beach; two shots were fired with lines attached. The violence of the gale carried the first to the leeward of the ship; the second shot carried and fastened the line to the ship; with it a large line was soon hauled off, and subsequently the life car was hauled through the terrific and foaming surf to the ship. In the life car embarked from two to four persons at a time, and with another line the loaded car was hauled to the shore with its load of passengers tightly enclosed within it, through the surf, and safely landed.
>
> "On the first day 120 persons were landed unharmed, with one single exception, which, as the last car left the ship at night, he [the anxious passenger] jumped, as was foreseen, the surf immediately washed him off, and he was lost. The next morning the remaining passengers were landed in like manner, during the time no boat could reach or land from the ship."

Dr Newell's persistence in Congress paid off. He is considered by some historians to be the father of the new U.S. Life-Saving Service.

In 1854, Congress voted more money to improve the service by hiring a superintendent for each coast, New Jersey and Long Island. In addition, a keeper was hired for each station.

The Underwriters and Insurers had formed an organization known as the Life Saving Benevolent Association (LSBA), incorporated under the laws of New York State. They acted as agents for the government and had the stations built and equipped. When the government money wasn't quite enough, they made up the difference. They issued a silver lifesaving medal and the sum of $25 (a large amount of cash in 1850) to John Maxon for his leadership in the Ayrshire rescue. It was he who fired the mortar.

The LSBA has given out awards to deserving rescuers through the years. They still exist today. They also paid volunteer lifesavers to unload the ships' cargoes and put them on trains for New York. The volunteers got paid after the people had been removed from the wreck. In this way the Underwriters managed to average about 85% recovery on their insured cargos. Wreckmasters, appointed by the state, were often also the keepers of the stations. They had the additional job of securing salvaged goods and keeping them from being stolen by beachcombers, who always managed to attend shipwrecks.

The Civil War froze all improvements to the system from 1862-1865. By 1871 it became obvious that the government needed to have hired hands on the beaches during the bad winter months. Superintendents were appointed in charge of the districts and they set about hiring crews for the stations. The winter of 1871-72 found these men in place and working. In other words, the paid U.S. Lifesaving Service started in 1871. The District Superintendent would make the rounds of the station areas and the crew found their way to him for their pay.

Soon the U.S. Life-Saving Service had spread to all the coasts and the Great Lakes. The men were lionized by the press and adored by the public for their heroic role is saving lives of those in peril at sea. Newspapers called them "Storm Warriors."

Many of the early shipwrecks attended by volunteers are not well documented. The volunteers did their jobs and went home. Perhaps someone wrote down the incident and a brief account of what happened. The Life Saving Benevolent Association has some records, but they are far from complete.

Ships Fear Fire More Than Water

by Carolyn Matthews
(Volume 8, Issue 1)

The year was April, 1853 when the Ocean Wave called into the Port of Kingston to load passengers, freight, as well as cordwood for her boiler fuel. She was a fine passenger steamer of the mid-19th century, built in Montreal to trade between New York and Hamilton, Ontario. Her passage was slow as she made stops at most of the ports along the way. Steamships, at this time, used fat fuel under the boilers and carried logs full of inflammable sap piled up on deck. This gave quick and plentiful heat that maintained the steam pressure required by the ship's engines but, together with any freshly-painted wooden surfaces, presented a considerable fire hazard on board.

The vessel was loaded, and sailed before midnight. By approximately one o'clock in the morning she was twenty-three miles from Kingston and close to two miles off the Duck Islands when the purser was told of a fire. Flames were already leaping up from the boiler room. Fanned by the winds that blew from the northwest, they spread with abandon to consume everything in their path. The heat was intense; fire spreading so rapidly that the crew could not launch their lifeboats carried on deck above the burning cabins. They, and the passengers, tried desperately to reach for the water buckets in attempts to quell them, but the flames had already devoured the entire cabin walls on which the fire buckets hung.

Within twenty minutes, the ship's cabins were a flaming furnace that lit up the sky for many miles around; those living on the nearby Duck

Islands saying that they were able to read by the light from the burning ship.

The two schooners, the Emblem and the Georgina, steaming near Duck Islands about this time, were attracted by the schooner's terrible plight by the brilliance of the sky lit up all about them. The captain thrust the Ocean Wave's engines into full steam and headed it toward the flaming ship to see if there was anything any of them could do to save the people on board.

The daring runs made by the sailors from the two schooners toward the blazing Ocean Wave have become legendary: sailors risked their lives repeatedly in the fiery blast of the vessel being consumed, in their attempts to take the people off the burning ship. In the end, twenty-one people survived, and twenty-eight died. The Ocean Wave sank, along with her cargo of 3000 barrels of flour, several hundred bags of seed grain, 300 kegs of butter, 60 barrels of potash, a large number of hams, as well as some general package freight. It was a tremendous loss in both lives and property, and presented a staggering blow to the Lake Ontario marine shipping interests of those days. But it did nothing at that time to pave the way for safer navigation in the following years. No new methods of attempting to change the conditions contributing to a fire hazard were implemented.

In Canada, prior to 1882, the government had done little to enhance safety on it's seas and waterways and the young country suffered tremendous loss of life, ships and property, the *Ocean Wave* but one among untold numbers. The tragic loss of life throughout the early years of the 1880s included two hundred and twenty-six in 1882, one hundred and fifty-seven in 1883, and one hundred and sixty in 1884. The honourable A. W. McClellan, minister of Marines and Fisheries, and William Smith, his deputy minister, became active, organizing the nucleus of a system under the authority of the government. Several stations were established, including one on Main Duck Island.

By 1897, Canada had one hundred and eighty-four light stations, two hundred and thirty-five lights, seventeen keepers, three lightships, two fog whistles, eleven fog horns, five bell buoys, and two gas buoys. Most were positioned on the Great Lakes, considered to be some of the most difficult navigable waterways in the world. Poor charting was the first serious problem in the early years, but the greatest difficulty was the lack of sea room: when ships ran for shelter looking for artificial harbours, they often missed and struck rocks, sand banks and piers. They encountered sudden gales that swept anchored vessels fore and aft and forced the crew into the rigging, to cling there until they perished in cold seas that swept over them, or were rescued, often against all odds. Feverish government activity took place up until 1897 when lighthouses increased from two hundred and twenty-seven to seven hundred and eighty-three.

In 1887, the lighthouse that was established at Main and False Duck Islands on Lake Ontario was built to accommodate a Keeper and his family, stationed there to aid sailors and prevent their grounding on the many rocky shoals that proliferated along its shores. At times, the islands also housed an occasional family, an idle visitor, witnesses too, to the violent destruction of many a Great Lake freighter destroyed in the fury of a great fire, dashed to oblivion on rocky shores, lost in the labyrinthine channels and in fog.

The lonely lighthouse station was inhabited by a keeper who was required to be fit, a master of boat craft, skilled in the art of surfing, and in wreck operations. The keeper selected his own crew.

It is the year 2000 and Coxswain Buell and his crew are on their search and rescue patrol among the Thousand Islands. If they know the early history of this area, they must be grateful that the work they do takes place in this century, and not the mid-nineteenth. A wreck occurring was not usually discovered until the sullen light of morning, perhaps many hours after the ship had been struck. On discovery, a courier on horseback might urgently be dispatched to a local life station - if one existed at the time - perhaps a telegram sent, or a train taken to the site of the shipwreck. Horses may have been hitched to draw the boat wagon with its boat and the crew to the shore close to where the ship had foundered. They would launch their boat immediately into huge inland seas, straining themselves at the oars. The dangers at the time were many: seas might overwhelm the little lifeboat and put the oarsmen in danger; it could capsize. If it did, the men would try to cling to it while it shuddered over rocks and shoals as it ground itself up on the shore. Courage, and a desire to save one human life, or many, inspired them yesterday, and does so, today.

Today, the lighthouse on Main Duck Island is abandoned, the meandering path to it overgrown with no life surviving but for an occasional snake in the long grass that lies over the rocky substrata. Its function has been replaced: today, navigational charts are detailed and up-to-date, and most vessels that sail the river into Lake Ontario are equipped with sophisticated navigational aids and means of communications: radar, depth sounders, global positioning systems, loran C, VHF radio.

What meets the eyes of the crew patrolling in the modern Coast Guard cutter today is an entirely different universe from the one that met the eye of the early French explorers. At the discovery of the Thousand Islands in 1650, the governor of New France could not find anything agreeable about them but their multitude 'an infinity of little islands of such number and variety that the most experienced Iroquois pilots sometimes lose themselves" (1. Endnote.)

Navigation along the river proved so difficult that the French planted a particular type of poplar along a channel that hugged the north shore of Lake Ontario, much like Hansel and Gretel leaving a trail of bread crumbs behind them so they would not get lost in the woods. Tragic shipwrecks of old are legion and have entered the lore and psyche of the local people here, and of sailors everywhere. Several hundred years later, the desperate tales are not forgotten.

Brockville, witness to some of the terrible wrecks, is built on the riverbanks opposite many of the Thousand Islands. It began as a series of little creeks and marshland, and by 1785, its few inhabitants saw a tree-lined path for wagons that stretched before and beyond it, skirting the edge of the swamps. Bateaux, and large and small scows crowded the river that jumped with black bass. In 1816 following the war of 1812, the river was surveyed and a zigzag line drawn through the middle of both river and lake that, for six months of every year, provided a marine highway to the West.

The year 1820 saw steamboats such as the Frontenac plying the river, allowing freedom of travel without dependency on the weather. It was a time of steam whistles, and large, gaily-coloured crowds gathered on the docks and wharves.

Islands, in popular imagination, create images of escape and seclusion, of romantic idylls and hideaway places. But almost two hundred years ago the images and purposes for these islands were entirely different: they were used strictly for utilitarian purposes, stripped of their forests and reduced to bare rock, cliffs and brush cover. They were inhabited by people that the Indians considered squatters: poor fishermen, wood cutters and boatmen, until the era of the mills.

A visitor, not long after this period, wrote about the Thousand Islands: "There is so much that is grand, weird, sublime and exhilarating in the scenery, and the balmy atmosphere of the majestic river that we need not wonder at the increase in intelligent people who repair to its placid waters in summer." (2. End note). Hotel and guesthouses were built; navigational lights and lighthouses were created and positioned, and channels explored, but the smaller ones long remained unknown. This was the beginning of a boom in the tourist industry among the Islands that, with interruptions, flourishes to this day.

In these early years, hunting and fishing, and the beautiful scenery attracted the tourists to the Thousand Islands. Father would be out hunting in the woods, the children playing on the riverbanks, and Mother sitting on the hotel verandah, gazing at the largely vacant islands. She wanted to own one. And because of her wish, and the desire of many others, the building of island homes and castles, of stone walls, gardens and orchards bloomed in the middle of the river. Craft were designed that were ideal for river transportation, the ubiquitous skiff being the most popular. It was constructed of oak and pine, was approximately twenty-one feet long, had with pointed ends, a sail, and a retractable folding centreboard. There was no rudder.

But the early popularity of the Thousand Islands was not sustained. The car allowed other exploration; the fires of 1911, 1912 demolished many of the grand houses and hotels. World War l intervened, and the Islands were closed when war was declared.

Today, this area of the St. Lawrence River is once again famed for its pleasure boating. The islands provide much of the attraction because of their abandoned homes and castles, places of historical curiosity, peace and beauty. The renting of houseboats has soared in popularity, but not without frequent mishap. Among their other responsibilities, the Coast Guard's rescue workers find themselves coming to the aid of those who get lost, run out of fuel, or who get stuck, sometimes because they believe that to drive a houseboat is no different from driving a car - nothing to it.

Maritime woes are different now: people generations later still lose themselves, get stranded, and their boats wrecked among the confusion of watery labyrinths formed by the islands, big and small, that rise up out or the water to scatter themselves with abandon all over the river. The majority today are pleasure boaters without adequate navigational tools, or boating experience, or who simply caught in sudden, severe storms keeping busy the lifeboat station crews at Cobourg, Kingston, Prescott, and Goderich.

Another Black Hole Filled: The Francis Metallic Surfboat

by Frederick Stonehouse
(Volume 6, Issue 1)

In 1848 Congress appropriated $10,000 to provide selected East Coast locations with "surfboats, rockets, carronades and necessary apparatus for the better preservation of life and property from shipwrecks..." While Congress did not provide funding for professional lifesaving crews, instead relying on local volunteers, the equipment proved useful in achieving Congress' intentions for the money. Additional allocations in subsequent years allowed Congress to send lifesaving equipment to other locations, including the Great Lakes. However, the lakes were not initially allocated any equipment other than forty-seven Francis metallic surfboats.

The boats were shipped to the lakes in the period of 1854 and 55. No beach wagons or other gear was provided. It was intended that government officials, lighthouse keepers or collectors of customs, would receive the boats with the understanding they would protect them and assure their proper use. In those instances where government officials were not available, private citizens could just post a bond and in turn receive a boat for local lifesaving. Records show that fourteen of the boats were sent to Lake Erie, nine to Lake Ontario, twenty-three to Lake Michigan and one to Lake Superior. None were sent to Lake Huron. One of the Lake Erie boats was kept at Marblehead, Ohio under the protection of Jared Keyes, the Marblehead lightkeeper. Whether or not he built a boathouse to shelter the craft is not known.

The Francis surfboat was a unique craft. Based loosely on the cedar surfboats used on the New Jersey shore, it was twenty-six and a half feet long, with a five and a half foot beam and had galvanized iron sides. The first models had wooden bottoms. Air tanks provided additional flotation. The wood bottom was later replaced with a metal one: the wood one deteriorated too quickly. The all-metal boats proved to be very tough and some stayed in service over fifty years, a testament to the design prepared by inventor and manufacturer Joseph Francis of the Novelty Iron Works in Brooklyn, New York. Although clearly a surfboat in design and function, local newspapers usually refer to them as lifeboats, somewhat complicating their history. The models sent to the lakes cost $450 each.

What is not known, however, is how these surfboats were used. What rescues did they perform? Who manned them? How successful were they? Thanks to Great Lakes shipwreck researcher David Swayze, who discovered the material for this short article, another black hole is at least partially filled.

The 350-ton bark *Empire*, hailing from Port Dover, Ontario, Canada, wrecked on Marblehead Point, approximately four miles from Sandusky, Ohio, on Lake Erie on May 5, 1857. Of the thirteen people aboard, all were lost except for captain Alexander Milligan and one crewman. The *Empire* was bound from Toledo, Ohio to Tonawanda, New York with a cargo of timber.

Luckily Sandusky was one of the cities that had received a surfboat, and the keeper of Sandusky Light was its guardian. He also was a witness to the wreck and commanded the surfboat in the rescue effort.

The storm caught *Empire* in the western part of the lake and its violence was so severe the captain was forced to come about, intending to shelter behind Kelly's Island. In the thick weather, however, he missed the island and did not realize his situation until he spotted the breakers off Peninsula Point, near Sandusky. The captain immediately hauled up tight in an effort to clear the point under all the canvas that the schooner could carry. All went well until 11 A.M., when a sudden blast of wind carried away the forestaysail sheet and jib sheet, causing the schooner to broach.

The captain immediately let go both anchors, which brought her head into the wind. The rest of the canvas quickly blew out into that screaming wind. The anchors held until 3 P.M. when the increasing waves caused them to drag. When it became apparent the ship was likely

Surfboat and lifeboat expert William D. Wilkinson notes that "We do know a little bit about the design of the Francis Life-Surfboat but there is, as Fred Stonehouse points out, much that we do not know. Hopefully, as more research is carried out we will find answers to the important questions that Fred raises." Drawing from Harper's New Monthly Magazine, *July 1851, Vol. III, No. XIV, page 168.* From the collection of William D. Wilkinson.

to sink, her two horses were pushed into the sea. The animals had been kept aboard to power the forward capstan used to haul the heavy timber balks aboard when loading. One horse drowned and the other reached the beach safely. The seas were now rolling so high they were sweeping over her deck. The crew fled to the rigging where they lashed themselves to prevent being blown off. Their situation was desperate at best. Shortly before 4 P.M. the schooner filled and capsized in deep water about 1,800 feet off Marblehead Light.

At the lighthouse, Keeper Jared Keyes quickly gathered a volunteer crew and launched the surfboat, himself taking the steering oar. As they tried to battle through the breakers, one oar snapped, then two more in quick succession. Without driving power, Keyes was obligated to turn back for the beach. But without the oars and lacking a disciplined crew, the surfboat and volunteers tumbled in the surf and all were washed ashore in an enormous wave. Luckily, none were injured.

Considering the lack of maintenance these Francis boats generally received, the breaking of the oars was almost to be expected. It was another example of the compelling need for a professional lifesaving service, both on the Great Lakes and around the entire United States.

Meanwhile, the schooner was not static. It was driven further down the shore by wind and wave. After getting new oars, Keyes and his crew launched again and this time were able to reach the schooner towing a line from shore. After getting the only two survivors into the surfboat, the crowd ashore hauled it in by the line. The captain was still conscious when taken into the boat but the crewman, Robert Moore, was insensible from the cold. The local newspaper was lavish in praise of Keyes and his crew, stating "...great praise is due to Captain Keyes and his brave boat's crew, who did all in their power to reach the wreck as speedily as possible, even at the imminent peril of their own lives."

The surfboat crew consisted of Keyes, J.A. Spencer, Richard Tichman, William A. Clemons, Charles Keyes, John Meacham, George Clark and John Burns. We know Charles Keyes was a son of the lightkeeper, but what do we know about William Clemmons? On June 19, 1876 Hubbard M., Lucian N. and H.J. Clemmons, all brothers, earned Gold Life Saving Medals for a rescue at Marblehead. Were they any relation to William? Jared Keyes was keeper at Marblehead from March 28, 1853 until November 19, 1858. He died in 1891.

The rescues performed on the Great Lakes using the early Francis boats are a fascinating part of American maritime history, in part because we know so little about them. The more we learn, the more we are impressed with the qualities of the Francis boat and the courage of the volunteer crews.

Growing Pains and Politics: White Head Life-Saving Station, 1873-1878

by David Gamage
(Volume 7, Issue 2)

The interpreted history of the U.S. Life-Saving Service is often presented through discussion of the interrelationships of three elements; rescues, regulations, and routines, and with reference to specific events such as the dates of the establishment of specific life-saving stations. However, the establishment of a life-saving station was not just an event. It was a process that began with selection of a location for a station and continued until this station became an effective and viable life-saving unit.

This process is described in "Growing Pains and Politics" from the perspective of a key individual, the first keeper of a life-saving station on an island on the coast of Maine. The personal journals of Keeper Horace Norton present a first person account of the first years of the new life-saving station on White Head Island that was established in 1874 during the early growth era of the U. S. Life-Saving Service within the Revenue Marine Bureau.

The Norton family acquired their 60 acres of the 70-acre White Head island in 1807. The White Head light station was already located on 10 acres at the easterly side of the island. Born on White Head in 1843, Horace Norton began writing a personal journal at age 17, which he continued until his death in 1911. He inherited the island land from his father and lived there with his wife and eight children until 1885. Norton earned a meager living from farming this land, from fishing and occasionally supplementing his income working in granite quarries on neighboring islands, salvaging wrecked vessels, temporary lightkeeping and piloting locally. He served one year as a White Head assistant lightkeeper.

At age 31 Norton was appointed keeper of the White Head Life-Saving Station. He was assigned the task to get this new and ill-equipped station manned and operational by the December 1, 1874 opening date. Revenue cutters delivered a few of the items for the station but often Norton rowed one and a half miles from White Head Island to Spruce Head on the mainland and then journeyed eight miles overland to Rockland to obtain supplies and equipment. His district superintendent was fully occupied with setting up six new life-saving stations from New Hampshire to Eastport, Maine, two of which were on islands more remote than White Head. Letters of instruction and documents for Keeper Norton were mailed to the mainland post office at Spruce Head. There was no telephone service on White Head Island until the late 1880s.

Horace Norton's accounts of the new White Head Lifesaving Station began with his journal entry of October 14, 1873, "The old revenue cutter came into the harbor today and brought an officer to select a site for the life-saving station to be built on White Head. He selected a place at Salt Works Cove and marked it by sticking two stakes in the ground."

The selection of locations for life-saving stations on the Maine coast began several months earlier. During late 1872 Capt. John Faunce and Lt. Louis Stodder of the Revenue Cutter Service traveled the length of the Maine coast on the cutter *McCulloch* to determine the need for establishing life-saving stations and to designate suitable sites. The report of this inspection is as follows in a local newspaper:

> "The sea coast of Maine from Portland to Eastport differs in almost every respect from that of the coasts of New Jersey, Long Island and Cape Cod, where life-saving stations have already been established. On the coast of Maine are numerous harbors with depth of water surpassing those of any other part of the United States, and numbers of islands stand boldly off the coast as watch-towers to passing vessels warning them of their danger. With this in mind, sites have been selected at points near entrances to harbors where the numerous vessels running upon the coast strive to make harbor in stormy weather. It is found

> upon a close examination of the coast and upon inquiry amongst sea-faring men, that it is at these points the greatest number of wrecks occur. Much information has been gathered from Mr. Leonard Grant, the pilot of the cutter *McCulloch*, who was shown upon the very stormy trip to Eastport and return to possess that knowledge which nothing but a close observation and years of experience upon the coast could have attained.
>
> "The trip to Eastport and return has been one in which a succession of gales and snowstorms has been encountered, and in which the inhospitable barriers of the coast have been clothed with all their terrors. The cutter *McCulloch* through the ability of her commander and officers has made the trip safely, stopping only when the vapor arising from the surface of the water precluded all possibility of running."

Seven potential locations for life-saving stations were identified, of which five were selected. A new life-saving station was recommended in the vicinity of White Head Island but "a specific location was not selected here owing to the very stormy weather, which has precluded the possibility of selecting the site."

White Head Island stands at the southern entrance to the 8-mile long Muscle Ridge Channel. Though hazardous for the presence of numerous ledges and small islands, this channel was a favored passage for sailing vessels and steamships entering or leaving West Penobscot Bay. The chain of Muscle Ridge islands bordering the eastern side of this provides vessels with protection from the easterly storm winds and waves of the open expanse of Penobscot Bay. To the north of White Head Island is Seal Harbor, a sheltered anchorage for vessels to await change in the weather or the lifting of the fog for which this area is noted. White Head Light Station, one of the first lighthouses in Maine, had marked the approach to the narrow channel entrance since 1805. Records of the number of vessel passages at White Head during the middle to late 1800s ranged from twenty to thirty thousand a year. Vessel strandings were frequent in the vicinity and particularly along the channel.

In early November 1873 contractor Andrew Newbert and a crew of five men came to White Head to commence building the life-saving station. Norton helped unload lumber at the harbor side of the island

and haul it overland to the station site at the southwest shore. Arrangements were made for the workers to board on the island at Norton's house. Construction was hampered by many stormy days with rain and snow. A near fatal accident involving one worker occurred on November 27. Norton records this in his journal: "Snow storm, gale of wind. Atwood fell from roof of station and hurt himself, taken up for dead, hauled to our house on handsled. Newbert went (to the mainland) in storm after doctor. Atwood had recovered when Dr. Wiggin arrived at 8 p.m. Wiggin stayed at our house all night."

On Jan. 1, 1874, the station structure was completed and the workers soon left the island. Perhaps to underscore the need for this station, the schooner Franklin wrecked three days later on the Browns Island ledges only a few hundred yards from this empty station building. Norton worked two days on the wreck. The vessel was a total loss.

In March, Norton went to the Customs Office in Rockland to apply for appointment to the keeper position. He "got a petition drawn up in support of his appointment and went around getting people to sign it."

On July 29, Captain J.H. Merriman of the Revenue Marine, and Customs Collector Mr. Crooker came to inspect the station and to finalize the lease agreement. Norton agreed to lease the Salt Works Cove site for $2 per year. District Superintendent John Richardson came to the island in September to inspect the station and to inform Norton he had been selected as station keeper. Norton's pay was $200 per year, effective when the station opened.

The 250-foot sidewheel steamship Cambridge grounded on Hay Island Ledge at the entrance to Seal Harbor on October 11. Keeper designate Norton went to assist during the successful three-day effort to unload and free this vessel. The life-saving station was not scheduled to open until December first. Norton did not have a crew of surfmen. The Revenue Cutter Levi Woodbury had delivered a square stern Higgins surfboat to the station. However, it was of no use, being unequipped and without oars. The Cambridge was the subject of Norton's first official wreck report.

Norton began recruiting surfmen in September but he could not officially sign them on because he had not received a copy of the Articles of Engagement. He borrowed a copy of regulations from the keeper of White Head Light Station for guidance in this. During October

In this early photograph of the White Head Lifesaving Station, taken on April 26, 1876, Keeper Horace Norton stands with his hand on the stern of the surfboat, while District Superintendent John Richardson, in civilian clothing at right, looks on. Photo use courtesy of David Gamage.

and November, with the help of his surfmen designates, he prepared the station for the open season. Norton journeyed to Rockland to obtain ten each of cots, mattresses, blankets, pillows, quilts, and chairs for the station, and eleven oars for the surfboat. He cut brush on the island to bank the station for winter. Norton and his crew installed in the first floor crew room the station stove and stovepipe in mid-November.

Norton cut and hauled two logs to make a launching slip for the surfboat since a launchway had not been provided. The tide zone in front of the station consisted of a preponderance of rocks and boulders that prevented safe launching and landing of the surfboat. In time a permanent launchway 250 feet in length would be constructed.

When the station opened on December first Norton wrote, "We went on duty today. I arranged the patrol to commence at 8 p.m. in accordance with Richardson's satisfaction. Divided six watches of two hours each, one man in a watch. Changed watches every night or so." The station was not yet fully equipped and was not completed inside. On December

4 the new boat wagon was delivered to Spruce Head. It was disassembled and transported to the station in the surfboat.

On January 14, 1875, the new keeper and his ill-equipped crew had their first shipwreck. The 250-foot steamer Georgia, running from Halifax, Nova Scotia, to Portland, became significantly off course at night in a snowstorm. At midnight the ship struck the Northern Triangle Ledges about six miles from the station. The 12 passengers and most of the crew of 47 departed the Georgia in lifeboats, leaving five of the crew and the pilot behind. The lifeboat the pilot was to command had fouled in the davits and capsized when it was lowered. The stern broke off the Georgia and the deck was awash forcing the six people on board to seek refuge on the ship's bridge. One of the lifeboats landed at White Head at 6 a.m. and it was then that the station crew was informed of the wreck. The surfboat was launched and reached the wreck site in about one hour. Heavy seas were running and the surfmen were obliged to watch their chances and to cautiously approach the wreck six times with one person from the wreck dropping on board each time. One of the passengers was so exhausted (hypothermia) that the crew was obliged to divert northerly 3 miles to Hewett Island where this victim was taken to a house and revived. The surfboat then returned to White Head where the shipwrecked persons were cared for until the next day when they were taken to Tenants Harbor in the surfboat, and then to Portland by the Revenue Cutter Dallas.

Five days later Supt. Richardson and Mr. Crooker came to the station. The crew received their first month's pay. Richardson told the local newspaper, "The crew was exercised in boat and mortar practice. They acquitted themselves handsomely and the superintendent expresses gratification in their proficiency. The lifeboat for the station had not yet been received, a surfboat being used in the trip to the wreck. Some other things are wanting to complete the full equipment of the station."

Norton wrote of this visit, "Richardson visited station and paid us one months pay. We fired the mortar for the first time. Shot parted from line and went over house and lodged in stone wall where I found it." (Apparently this was Norton's house. There was no stone wall within mortar range of the life-saving station and uneven terrain on either side of the station prevented its use as the "wreck" for the breeches buoy drill. It would be a few years later when a drill pole was constructed.)

Norton later notes, "we had a very cold winter and much ice, at one time ice field extended to Monhegan which was something I never saw before." Living conditions in this uninsulated station were difficult that first winter and with only one small stove for heat.

The White Head station was relatively inactive for the rest of the open season. After the May 1, 1875 closing there were numerous strandings during the closed season. Many times Norton summoned a crew of volunteers from nearby islands and the mainland for these incidents. Richardson expected Norton to submit monthly reports of passing vessels. It was not possible to see the channel from where the life-saving station was located, even from the watch platform on the roof, so Norton used White Head lightkeeper Isaac Grant's passing vessel records to complete his report.

Richardson advised Norton by letter in August that "he was in no case to employ two members of the same family as surfmen unless it was impossible to get a crew without doing so." This created a dilemma for Norton. Four of his surfman were relatives directly or by marriage. These were competent boatmen and who worked well together. But as Norton quoted in his journal, "Regulations must be lived up to."

On October 29, Norton received a letter from Richardson and Articles of Engagement for surfmen with "an order to ship a crew and go on duty for the 1875-76 season on November 1," not December 1 as was originally planned. Norton had only three surfmen available. Freeman Shea and Herbert Elwell, his No. 1 and No. 2 surfmen were on a fishing vessel at Cape Ann, Massachusetts. Norton signed on two substitutes, one of whom was his nephew who was only 15 years old at the time. Norton went to Rockland and successfully contacted Shea and Elwell by telegraph. They returned on Nov. 5 before Richardson arrived and would have discovered an underage surfman. The sixth surfman who signed on was Andrew Elwell. So now Norton had two Elwells, two Makers, one Rackliffe and one Shea whose wife was an Elwell-Rackliffe. And Norton's wife was an Elwell. So much for the regulations that "must be lived up to."

The station received two more boats during that winter. One was a 17-foot boat for use in the harbor and was kept at a landing place at North Point on the Seal Harbor side of the island. This boat was delivered to Rockland. Norton and two of his surfman rowed it 10 miles

The Coast Guard moved the boat room doors to the back of the 1874 station for its use as a storage facility, and further modifications took place after the building was struck by lightning. Photo use courtesy of David Gamage.

to Whitehead. This harbor boat was of great value because the crew no longer had to launch the surfboat and row nearly two miles around the island to reach the harbor and then to Spruce Head village to obtain supplies and mail. The second boat received was a new self-bailing lifeboat designed by Supt. Richardson. There was no place to store this lifeboat and it was received without oars or equipment so it was hauled out on the island and stored for the winter.

The 1876-77 open season brought more difficulties for Norton. This was a presidential election year, the year of the hotly contested Hayes vs. Tilden 1876 election. Problems began for Norton when Richardson told him in September to "ship a crew of Republicans for the coming open season." Norton did as he was told for fear of losing his appointment as keeper. At the outset he lost his most experienced surfmen. No. 1 Surfman Freeman Shea, though a Republican, refused to go along with this political scheme and quit in disgust. No. 2 Surfman Herbert Elwell refused to enroll in the Republican Party. Norton then proceeded to put together a crew of six new men who met Richardson's political qualifications.

To add further to his grief, Norton was asked by a prominent local citizen "if I had discharged my old crew and hired a new one who were Republicans. I told him yes. He was very indignant and reported our interview to the Rockland Opinion. The Opinion published an editorial in which he commented on these facts in a manner not complimentary to my new crew."

From the *Rockland Opinion*, November 3, 1876:

> "REPUBLICAN CIVIL SERVICE REFORM.
> "A Life-Saving Station Made a Political Machine.
>
> "The Republican party have got all the offices in train to do the utmost possible for it. Every little source of patronage is made to tell. But it is only recently that the lighthouse system and the life-saving service of the coast have been made a political machine. Previous administrations have universally considered that it was of greatest importance that the efficiency of the service should be maintained, at all hazards, whether those who hold subordinate positions in it belong to one party or another. The demoralizing rule of civil service which gives positions in reward for political services, rather than on account of the fitness of the appointee, has never been applied here, where it would manifestly be so dangerous. We cannot afford to have our lighthouses kept by numbskulls, even though they may be good political workers; it is of the highest importance that the first-class men be selected to man our life-boats, even if they cannot pack a caucus.
>
> "But the second administration of Grant has changed all this. Every Democrat that was in the service four years ago has now been displaced, and Republicans appointed, no matter how unfit. We have alluded to one case of this sort- that of the lighthouse-keeper on Mark Island, where the widow of a soldier

was turned out to make room for one of Eugene Hale's lackeys. We now hear a case in which the efficiency of the life-saving service has been sacrificed to gain a few votes for the Republican Party.

"The life-saving station at White Head was established one year ago, and has been the means of doing a great deal of good. A station of this kind is greatly needed there, and those employed should be experienced oarsmen and strong, able men. It is in charge of Capt. Horace Norton, who was appointed when the station was established. He is a gentleman well adapted to the place, and has always given great satisfaction to all who had occasion to need his services. He is a Republican, of course, but no one would think of objecting to the appointment of a Republican to the place, provided he is fit for it. Besides the captain there are six surfmen at the station. These are engaged by the captain. When the crew was made up, Capt. Norton selected his men with reference to their fitness, not their politics.

"The six surfmen were men who had passed their lives by the seashore or upon the ocean itself. All were strong, robust active men, and all thoroughly at home in a boat, with an oar in their grasp. As most of the seafaring men along the coast are Democrats, it is not perhaps surprising that of these six men five were Democrats. They are only employed during six months of the year, and were discharged on the first of May. When the time approached for commencing operations this season -the first of November - the men got notice from Captain Norton that their services would not be required. It was ascertained that a new crew had been engaged, all of whom were Republicans. One of them a cripple, unable to do a man's work; one of them is so timid in a boat that he does not dare to alone cross from Spruce Head to the main when the wind is fresh; two of them had scarcely ever handled an oar; none of them would be considered first-class men. But all vote the Republican ticket. One, who lives at South Thomaston, voted that way for the first time in his life last September. Was not that a pretty crowd to man a lifeboat! If they ever get out on the water someone will have to be out to save their lives.

> "When we learned the above facts, a representative of the Opinion called on Capt. Norton, to learn if it had been correctly represented to us. He admitted that the services of the men employed last season had been dispensed with, and that it was for political reasons. The new crew was inferior to the old one, but was as good as he could get without taking any Democrats. To the question, whether or not he considered that the right way to do business, he replied promptly and somewhat warmly, that he did not. He was not in favor of such a thing, but could not help himself. 'Why,' said he, 'in case Tilden is elected, I should of course expect to lose the place of captain: but if we did not draw party lines in the minor appointments, the Democrats would not then do so, and I might be employed as a surfman. Now they will kick me out altogether unless they are fools.'
>
> "He said that he had received orders from the commissioner to be sure and have seven Republican votes from the station, and had unwillingly complied, and took men recommended by Republican politicians. One of the old crew was a Republican, but he had discharged him so as to let the politicians have a crew of their own choosing throughout. And he intimated very strongly that he thought they had made a mess of it. He thought the lighthouse commissioner had got his orders from William P. Frye, member of congress from the Second District.
>
> "Seamen, you who are liable to be wrecked in that dangerous locality will you vote with a party that deliberately sacrifices your safety for the sake of getting votes? On the same principle, may not the next step be to give instruction to the life-saving crew not to attempt to save the lives or property of Democrats?"

This letter appeared four days before the presidential election and the obvious intent of the local newspaper was to obtain more votes for Tilden, the Democratic candidate. This was the infamous election of 1876 in which both sides claimed victory and that was finally settled in March by the Compromise of 1877, giving the presidency to Hayes.

A second letter appeared in the Opinion soon after the election. "The Republicans are not feeling so jubilant as they did, especially the men at the life-saving station on White Head, who celebrated Hayes's election three weeks ago, and are now sick with disgust to think what damn fools they made of themselves."

Norton and his crew believed that they would lose their jobs if the Democrat Tilden were elected. Norton wrote in his journal, "The whole winter was passed in uncertainty as to who was elected President of the U.S. States. We took the *Boston Journal* at the station and paid 64 cents for six months. It took all winter to settle the election and when near March fourth we learned that Hayes was declared elected we were greatly relieved."

On a brighter side, the life-saving station living areas were plastered and sheathed during November to provide insulation. A second stove was installed to give much needed heat for the second floor. In the spring of 1877 a new boathouse with 130-foot launchway was built at North Point to contain the lifeboat and the harbor boat. This second launchway provided a much-needed alternate landing place for the surfboat when storm seas prevented safe landing at the more exposed main launchway at the life-saving station.

At the end of the open season in 1877 Richardson instructed Norton to "get rid of" two of his surfmen. Norton took this a step further and got rid of two more. When the station opened the following season Norton had selected a crew of his choice including Freeman Shea and Herbert Elwell and two others from his first crew before the election year Republican crew fiasco.

Sumner Kimball and Treasury Secretary John Sherman visited the life-saving and light stations on White Head on July 11, 1877. They were accompanied by Capt. Walker of the Lighthouse Board, Capt. Patterson of the Coast Survey, and Web Hayes, son of President Hayes. Norton wrote nothing of what took place during this visit but he did mention their departure on the 160-ft Revenue Cutter Grant when this distinguished party received a first hand introduction to the hazards of the Muscle Ridge Channel. Norton wrote, "The Grant struck Lower Gangway Ledge and stove in her plates. Had to run her on the flats on the north side of Spruce Head. The cutter was detained for several days." After two attempts to pull the Grant off the flats she was finally pulled free by the Lighthouse Tender Iris and towed to the South Marine Railway at Rockland. There the Grant was nearly wrecked again on the railway when a link of the hauling chain broke and she ran back down the track, getting hung up until the next high tide. Kimball told Norton not to bother submitting a wreck report concerning the ledge incident and that he would take care of it himself. Web Hayes had seen enough and returned home. Kimball and colleagues continued the tour to the West Quoddy station and back on the Iris.

Norton was lenient with his crew. His No.1 Surfman of the Republican crew went absent without leave for a week and Norton failed to report this. He covered the absence with an alternate surfman. Norton wrote of this, "We were inspected by Capt. Walker and Lt. Shoemaker. Caught up in rather bad shape and I got a reprimand in reference to our system of deception." Norton also stated earlier in his journal he "made sure his men got all the time off they were owed, and a little more."

On January 10, 1878, Norton wrote in his journal, "I got orders by letter from Richardson to have two patrolmen out at a time. Hereafter it will be four hours for a patrol. One of the severest gales tonight ever known. I stood watch all night, as I didn't want to put too many hours on to my crew." This new patrol implementation was deemed necessary because of the inappropriate location of the station. It was not possible to observe for vessels in any part of the Muscle Ridge Channel from the watch platform on the station roof. In later years a watchtower with adequate view would be constructed on high ground a short distance from the station.

During the January northeasterly storm a schooner dragged anchor and grounded at high tide on a ledge at the western side of the Seal Harbor. Norton and his crew worked five days to get this vessel off the ledge. They first lightened the vessel by removing nearly 100 barrels of flour and other cargo but were unable to kedge the empty vessel from the ledge after several attempts and three days of effort. So then they took a different tack; they removed the ledge from beneath the vessel. Using skills learned from working in the local granite quarries two of the surfmen drilled and split rock at low tide from under the side and keel for two more days to finally free the vessel from this ledge.

In February 1878, Norton received a letter from Richardson about possible transfer of the service to the Navy. Norton writes, "I went to Rockland today to see Deputy Collector Crooker in compliance with the letter from Richardson. Richardson wanted me to get Crooker to assist in getting up a remonstrance against transfer of the Life Saving Service to the Navy." On March 6, "I wrote an article for the Rockland Gazette, carried to Rockland and had it published in the Rockland Opinion, an article remonstrating against transfer of the service from the Treasury Department to the Navy Department. Got home late at night." This was political activity that was not the responsibility of the keeper, nor should he have gotten involved. Norton was never told otherwise. He just followed Richardson's orders, orders that required him to leave the station during open season.

In this matter Norton wrote in July, "Congress acted favorably on a bill to reorganize the Life-Saving Service and increased the pay of keepers from $200 to $400 per year. The active season has been extended from six to eight months and is to commence on September 1 and continue to May 1. Keepers have been vested with the power of Inspector of Customs and were required to take another oath of office."

After the station opened for the 1877-78 season Norton wrote in his journal, "We received a barometer and a thermometer and the crew are to write down readings four times a day. We are to give attention to mortar drill and other drills also to resuscitate drowned men. Inspected by Lt. Shoemaker and Lt. Sawtelle, found all right and crew fully up to mark."

From the beginning with two stakes in the ground and after four years of growing pains and politics the White Head Life-Saving Station was at last fully operational and manned with a crew of competent surfmen, this accomplished to a great extent through the continual efforts of Keeper Horace Norton.

The journals of Horace Norton provide a unique insight into the establishment of a life-saving station and of the many challenges overcome by this new keeper, and by his district superintendent to transform an empty building to become a viable, fully functional unit of the United States Life-Saving Service.

Horace Norton resigned his keeper position in June 1882. He gave no reason for this in his journal. Norton then signed on as a surfman for the next two open seasons. He declined to re-engage for the 1884-85 season. In October 1885, Norton and his family left White Head and moved to Westbrook, Maine where they lived until his death in 1911.

Freeman Shea was appointed to replace Norton as keeper of the

White Head Life-Saving Station. One of his first tasks as the new keeper was to search for a drowning victim, his own son Wilbert Shea, who was run down by the steamer Penobscot near the lighthouse. Freeman Shea, No. 1 surfman of the first crew at this station, served 29 years as White Head keeper until his death in September 1911. Surfman Alonzo Maker, Shea's No. 1 surfman was appointed keeper and served until his retirement in 1918.

Superintendent John Richardson continued his career in the Life-Saving Service until his death on June 13, 1896. Keeper Shea was offered this superintendent position, but refused. Silas Harding, keeper of the station at Jerrys Point (NH) was appointed district superintendent.

Norton's former No. 2 Surfman, Herbert Elwell, was appointed keeper of the new Burnt Island Life-Saving Station in 1891 at a site selected by Shea and Richardson. The underage alternate, Francis Snow, eventually engaged as a surfman at White Head where he served for fifteen years.

The lifesaving station became the White Head Lifeboat Station following the creation of the U.S. Coast Guard in 1915. In 1921 a Chatham style barracks replaced the original station. A double bay boathouse equipped with an iron rail launchway was constructed at the cove at the northeastern end of the island. A new watchtower was erected near the lighthouse and beside the 1903 Weather Service storm signal tower. The Burnt Island and White Head lifeboat stations operated in tandem as Group White Head. In 1954 the White Head station was closed. The crew and boats were relocated to the mainland at Rockland and became the present day Coast Guard Station Rockland.

The 1921 barracks and boathouse remain today on the island. The preserved 1874 life-saving station still stands at Saltworks Cove where it continues to serve as a reminder of the surfmen and keepers of this and other life-saving stations and who were the U.S Life-Saving Service.

SECTION III:
The Golden Era

Discretion Is the Better Part of Valor

by Frederick Stonehouse
(Volume 6, Issue 3)

When we think of the old U.S. Life-Saving Service, the words that immediately come to mind are courage, bravery, daring and guts. Perhaps put most simply, discretion is not normally associated with the old lifesavers. However, on November 12, 1880, discretion was very much the watchword on Lake Erie.

On that date the small 57-foot, 40-ton British schooner George W. Mowbray, bound from Montreal for Fort William on Lake Superior, ran into Erie, Pennsylvania, for shelter from a roaring northwest storm and snowstorm. On entering the harbor well before dawn she dropped her anchors, but the powerful winds and surging seas soon parted the cables, and the helpless schooner was driven hard onto an old crib pier near the west breakwater. The crew of six quickly scrambled onto the crib and eventual safety, barely escaping with their lives. The schooner was pounding heavily against the old crib and it was only a matter of time before she went to pieces.

The crew of the Erie Life-Saving Station learned of the wreck at 5 a.m. and immediately went to her aid in their lifeboat. When they reached the schooner and saw the crew was safely off, the lifesavers went into the hold to check the cargo. When they realized what it was, they deserted the ship at what must have been a record pace. Deep in the schooner's hold was a consignment of forty tons of nitro glycerin intended for the Canadian Pacific Railway for use in building the trans-Canadian railroad. Considering the severe pounding action of the waves,

The men of the Erie (PA) Life-saving Station, here in a relaxed moment in front of their 1875-type station, would never forget what they discovered in the hold of the George W. Mowbray *on November 12, 1880. Photo courtesy of Ralph Shanks and* The United States Life-Saving Service: Heroes, Rescues and Architecture of the Early Coast Guard, *page 171.*

the lifesavers and much of the town waited in apprehension for what everybody assumed would be a massive explosion. It never happened. The following day the lake calmed, and the volatile cargo was safe.

Captain Mellwain of the Mowbray later told a local reporter the nitro glycerin was valued at $50,000. The small schooner had been involved in the dangerous trade for five years without previous accident. Hauling such dangerous cargo was usually done "on the quiet," without telling anybody what was in the hold. One tug captain remembered being offered $1,000 to tow the schooner through the Soo Canal but was never told what exactly he would have at the other end of the tow rope.

When the lake quieted that next day, a scow was carefully brought alongside and the cargo gingerly transferred. The nitro scow was later safely anchored three miles from town until another schooner arrived to haul it away. No chances were to be taken until it was gone from Erie. Then other lake towns could worry about it.

Once the explosive was removed from the Mowbray, the lifesavers, together with a tug, several boats from the Revenue Cutter Perry and the U.S. steamer Michigan attempted to pull the schooner off the crib, but were unable to do so. The schooner eventually went to pieces.

For the Erie Life-Saving crew, it was a wreck long remembered. Not for a dangerous rescue performed, but instead for their discrete retreat.

Gone But Not Forgotten: A Great Lakes Life-Saving Station

by William D. Peterson, Ph.D
(Volume 4, Issue 1)

A falling barometer and increasing easterly winds signaled the end of the day on September 8, 1885. In these conditions Lake Huron turned from tranquil blue to its mean spirited gray. At the Sturgeon Point Life-Saving Station, Michigan, surfmen left for evening beach patrols making notes to themselves to be extra vigilant with the worsening conditions. By the early evening the wind reached the "fury of a hurricane." Unknown to the Life-Saving crew the schooner barge *Genessee Chief*, and her crew of seven at anchorage at Black River were in trouble. Her anchors were slipping and although she was flying a distress flag, the tugs at Black River were unable to get to her due to worsening conditions on the Lake. Sometime near midnight, knocking on the door of the Sturgeon Point Station was heard over the raging storm. Keeper Eugene Motley and the surfmen not on patrol gathered as a messenger from Black River described the bad situation unfolding ten miles north of the station.

Keeper Motley quickly dispatched part of his crew to secure a team of horses to haul the surfboat and gear to Black River. He then burned Coston flares at the station to recall his patrols. By dawn the Sturgeon Point crew had traveled to Black River and launched their boat, "in a tremendous sea that would have appalled less stout hearted men." In the early morning of September 9, after working all night, the Sturgeon Point Life-Savers drew alongside the schooner, Keeper Motley and his crew removed the endangered mariners from the swamped schooner and started the difficult return trip to shore. Once safely on shore they dried their clothes and rested at a local hotel. By the morning of September 10, 1885, the storm had "abated somewhat" and the life-saving crew and the crew of the *Genesee Chief* were hard at work making repairs and pumping out the barge. With the help of the Life-Saving Service the Chief was underway again by 2 p.m. September 10, 1885. Just another day's work for the United States Life-Saving Service at Sturgeon Point, Michigan.

Among Michigan's most prominent landmarks are its lighthouses. These structures are majestic reminders of Michigan's glorious maritime tradition. The Sturgeon Point Light is located between Oscoda and Alpena, just north of Harrisville. The seventy foot tower and adjoining Keeper's home were completed during the fall of 1869. Due to the lateness of the season when completed, the light went unlit until the spring of 1870. Today the light and the keeper's quarters attract visitors from all over Michigan. The site is run by the Alcona Historical Society which restored the light in the early 1980s and now maintains a small museum in the old keeper's home.

The lighthouse is a romantic and glamorous reminder of the past importance of this site, but what is now gone from Sturgeon Point is an equally, perhaps more powerful reminder of a bygone era. Just to the south of the light once stood the Sturgeon Point Life-Saving Station. This tidy compound of building housed, by comparison to the lighthouse, a larger complement of government employees. While the lighthouse required a single keeper, a life-saving station had a keeper and a crew of seven or eight men. Often the families of both keepers lived at these installations.

Because it was constructed of wood, the Sturgeon Point Life-Saving Station was unable to stand up to time and the elements as well as its brick neighbor. After abandonment by the government in 1941, time and vandalism quickly took its toll and by the end of the 1960s there was nothing left of this once exciting establishment. Now an empty field is the only thing which reminds the lighthouse visitor of the old Life-Saving Station at Sturgeon Point. Nevertheless, the importance of this vanished Life-Saving Station and others like it cannot be forgotten.

While the section of Lake Huron between Alpena and Tawas is not well known for its treachery, the heads of the Life-Saving Service determined there was sufficient danger, as well as large volumes of shipping traffic, to merit several first class life-saving facilities. The station built at Sturgeon Point was an 1875-type designed by USLSS architect Francis W. Chandler. It went into operation in September of 1876 as Station Number Three within USLSS District Nine. It later became station five in district ten. Perley Silverthorn was the first Keeper, followed in 1881 by Harry Broadwell. In March of 1884, Eugene Motley took command of the station. District Superintendent Jerome Kiah appointed James E. Henderson keeper of the Sturgeon Point Life-Saving Station at 10:30 p.m. on October 4, 1885. Henderson held his position until 1915.

The work of the Life-Saving Service crews was hazardous and seasonal. They pay scale did not necessarily reflect the importance of the job, nor the dangers. During the month of July 1897, the Keeper and the crew of the Sturgeon Point Station were paid the following.

J.E. Henderson, Keeper $75.80
Addison Silverthorn, Surfman $65
Louis Cardy, Surfman $65
William Hugell, Surfman $65
William Hilliard, Surfman $65
Samuel Newell, Surfman $65
Henry Sweet, Surfman $65
George Cuyler, Surfman $65
William Finch, Surfman $65

The crew of the Sturgeon Point Life-Saving Station made its first response to a distressed vessel on December 12, 1877. The crew of the schooner *Monterey*, commanded by Captain Merrick, was saved along with the ship. Unfortunately, a cargo of lumber valued at $5,000 was lost. It was fairly quiet at the station for the next several years. Indeed, the crew of Sturgeon Point did not make it into the Annual Reports of the Life-Saving Service until September 3, 1878 when they helped pump out the schooner *Vampire*. A month later they took five crewmen off of the scow *E.K. Kane*. The next day, October 4, they helped pump the vessel out and refloat her. It was in these types of rescues and situational responses that the presence of the USLSS was felt the most. They were good Samaritans of sorts, always ready to lend a helping

The men of the Sturgeon Point Life-Saving Station perform a breeches buoy drill on the Lake Huron shore. Photo courtesy of the Alcona Historical Society.

hand. In this way, through their lending of manpower, they were able to save U.S. shipping and insurance companies millions of dollars.

The burning of the steamer *Marine City* was the only total loss ever witnessed by the Sturgeon Point crew. Keeper Perley Silverthorn wrote in his daily log that August 29, 1880 was a calm day, with moderate winds out of the northeast. That season's crew consisted of Surfman Addison Silverthorn, H.S. Broadwell, Donald McDonald, B. Frederick, W.O. Burk and J. Greenman (this name may not be correct). During daylight hours in calm weather, the USLSS regulations permitted the absence of the crews from the station as long as one crewman stayed to keep the day watch and ring the alarm in the case of an accident. Crews were required to return immediately if the weather turned bad or they heard the alarm bell.

On August 29, 1880, the crew was apparently off picking berries when the *Marine City* caught fire around 3:30 p.m. Surfmen Broadwell was keeping watch at the station. According to the keeper's journal Addison Silverthorn saw the fire and sounded the alarm, all seven of the crew returned to the station immediately launching the surfboat. The *Marine City* was burning three miles from the station. The Sturgeon Point Life-Saving crew arrived second on the scene at 4:10 p.m. behind either the tug *Grayling* or *Vulcan* (one newspaper says *Grayling*, P. Silvertorn's journal entry says *Vulcan*). Once on the scene of the fire they picked up five survivors, however the fire claimed nine lives. The Sturgeon Point crew spent the rest of the week attending to the grisly task of looking for bodies and either burying them or holding them for relatives to pick up.

On November 26, 1883, the crew of Sturgeon Point rowed ten miles in a heavy northwest gale to take seven passengers off the schooner *Hamilton J. Mills*. On April 25, 1889, after a three hour row of ten miles, the crew of the Sturgeon Point Station came to the aid of the schooner *White Star*. The vessel was saved and the efforts of the Sturgeon Point crew prompted a letter from the owner of the schooner, L.L. Slyfield:

> Sir: On April 24th the schooner *White Star*, valued at ten thousand dollars, partly loaded and in tow of a tug ran ashore on Black River Island Reef, and there being some sea at the time was in great danger of pounding bottom. Captain J.E. Henderson, of the Sturgeon Point Life-Saving Station, some ten miles distant, discovered our situation and with his crew came promptly to our relief. After they had worked some thirty hours in running about two thousand feet of line to the tugs and assisting to lighten the schooner, we succeeded in getting her off. Too much credit can not be given these resolute men, for had they not been at hand our vessel could not have been released before a gale of wind would have overtaken us, and the chances then would have been against floating her at all.
>
> Yours respectfully,
> L.L. Syfield

This was not the only time the crew of the Sturgeon Point Station received praise from those they had helped. On October 5-8 of 1889, the crew helped secure the schooner *Kingfisher* on the shore during a northeast gale. The vessel master, Edward T. Drake, wrote USLSS tenth District Superintendent Captain Jerome G. Kiah the following letter:

> Dear Sir: I wish to inform you of the gallant services rendered me by CAPT. J.E. Henderson and crew, of the Sturgeon Point Station, on October 5, when my fishing schooner was driven

ashore by a fierce northeast gale. They gave such prompt and efficient aid that the schooner and her cargo were saved from destruction.

Edward T. Drake

What would life at Sturgeon Point have been like in the 1880s? The regulations of the USLSS divided activities at stations into specific duties for each day of the week, excluding Sunday. The schedule for all stations across the country was exactly the same. If you were to visit Sturgeon Point during the active season at any time, you could expect the following to be going on around you. On Mondays the crew practiced with the beach cart (apparatus), inspected their equipment, and made necessary repairs. Often the northern Michigan weather made the daily practice near impossible, as on November 5, 1885: "Practice ground covered with water making it too wet to practice beach drill went to north poast (sic) with surf boat, poast are all right. J.E. Henderson, Keeper."

Drilling with the surfboats and lifeboats occupied Tuesday. Early in November of 1885 the crew assisted the schooner *Snow Drop* at Harrisville. By Tuesday November 3, their help was no longer needed and Keeper Henderson noted the passage of the day: "Day watch surfman Pearson and Newell Boat Practice I went to Harrisville today and offered our assistance to the owners of *Snow Drop*, he thanked me and said he had engaged a crew of men and had it already (pumped) out."

On Wednesday the crew exercised with signal flags. Often the Keeper made a simple recording in his daily log which indicated the practice went as scheduled. Yet more beach cart practice was scheduled on Thursday. On Thursday May 18, 1915, near the end of his career, James Henderson made the following journal entry: "Practiced with surf boat. Went to Harrisville with surf boat for Government supplies. From Grand Haven Mich. 2 boxes hardware; 3 boxes paint; 1 box soap; 1 box glass; 1 bbl glassware; 1 crate yunce board [? - illegible]; 1 bbl brooms; 1 bbl. Mopsticks; 1 roll oilcloth."

Training for the resuscitation of the apparently drowned occupied Friday and cleaning the station took up Saturday. Sunday was a day of rest.

The beach cart drill and the surfboat practice were popular among the nearby residents of the Sturgeon Point Station. The beach cart drill

Surfmen pose during the breeches buoy drill at Sturgeon Point Life-Saving Station. Photo courtesy of the Alcona Historical Society.

was dramatic since it involved a simulated rescue using the Lyle gun and breeches buoy. On at least two occasions, the crew of the Sturgeon Point Station were asked by the community to give demonstrations of their talents. One such request was during June of 1903 when Matthew Hale, President of the I.O.O.F. Picnic Association asked the crew for a demonstration. The District Superintendent gave the crew permission to perform the exhibition on July 30, 1903 as long as the government incurred no expense as a result. A request for an exhibition from O.H. Smith of the Huron Shores Sunday Shores Association for their picnic on July 14, 1910 was denied. The reason for the denial was that the picnic was too far from the station.

The USLSS considered the beach patrol its most important duty. During these patrols the surfmen would look for vessels in distress or running too close to shore. Many groundings were avoided by surfmen lighting their flares and warning vessels off. On November 4, 1885 Keeper Henderson made the following entry noting the practice of the signals, the health of a crewman, and difficulties with the patrol clock system:

> Day watch, Surfman Hugall and Reed Code Signals. Surfman J.L. Cardy had his hand lanced today the doctor think he may lose a finger on account of losing the joint oil.

The North Clock time detector No 29.94 stopped at 12 a.m. must have been about the time I found Surfman Silverthorn on watch from 12 to 4. North patrol did not notice it being stopped so there is two impressions on the dial at 12 of the short and long patrol. I questioned the crew closely in regards to the matter Surfman Silverthorn said after leaving short post on return to station he stopped to get a drink throwing watch over his shoulder and I think the sudden jar started it running as that would have been about 3 a.m.

J.E. Henderson Keeper

Henderson's log is full of entries in which he mentions the time clock system continually giving him grief. The above journal entry mentions the necessity of medical attention. Every year surgeons from the U.S. Marine Hospital Service inspected the keepers and the crews of the Life-Saving Service. Examination rooms were not easy to find at Sturgeon Point and in July 1882, the surgeon examined the crew, "in cellar behind" the station. If any were found to be unfit they were immediately discharged. On only two occasions were crew members at Sturgeon Point discharged for being physically unfit. In May of 1878

It was 1917 when this photo was taken and the Sturgeon Point life-savers now wore the uniform of the newly-formed United States Coast Guard. *Photo courtesy of the Alcona Historical Society.*

District Superintendent Captain Joseph Sawyer ordered one surfman discharged. In October 1882 Keeper Broadwell was ordered to discharge surfman Spencer Showers? (I couldn't quite make out the name in the records) by the district superintendent as he was "reported physically unfit for duty."

The USLSS realized that alertness was required of the crews as they stood their watches. However, their comfort was not much of a concern. In April of 1902 Jerome Kiah sent a letter to the Duluth Station keeper and forwarded a copy to all "no seat for watchmen in your station lookout, either day or night." As to the comfort of the crews during the bitter cold watches kept in the spring and late fall Kiah had this to say: "Referring to your letter of 2nd ultimo, requesting permission to purchase stove for lookout at your station, you are informed that a stove for the purpose mentioned will not be allowed at government expense. There will be no objections to using such a stove if the crew desires to provide one at their own expense."

The USLSS was frugal in the allocation of equipment. In May of 1902 Jerome Kiah informed Keeper Henderson that the "English model lifeboat at the Ottawa Point (Tawas) will be transferred to our station at the first favorable weather for sailing." In July of that year, Chas. Conklin was sold the old lifeboat for $16. In 1910, the District Superintendent told Henderson to place posters at the Harrisville Post Office, the Station, and in one other highly visible place. These posters advertised "the sale of the Higgins and Gifford surfboat at your station, which has been condemned by the board of survey."

Not all of the work performed by the Life Saving crew at Sturgeon Point was as glamorous and dramatic as assisting mariners. Much of their work involved maintaining and improving the station. At numerous times in the course of the station's history there were major building projects undertaken by the crew. During the operating season of 1883, Keeper Broadwell recorded in his daily log that the crew was busy building a new boathouse. He wrote on October 31 and November 1 the crew spent the day "setting out timbers for boat house" and "getting timbers near a boat house." They started framing the new boathouse on November 2, and finished shingling it November 24.

In April of 1884 the station received a workshop on the side of the boathouse. In June Keeper Motley made the following entry: "Built the new chimney on rear of station in place of the current one which was cracking and was unsafe. He [a bricklayer] also repaired the one on front of station, in which a few bricks which turned too soft had crumbled away."

In July of 1887 the crew built a new set of stairs outside the station. Other work included the addition of two dormer windows in the crew's quarters during the winter of 1897. A letter from District Superintendent Jerome Kiah dated December 24, 1897 details the extent of the addition:

> Authority is hereby given you in the view of the immediate necessity therefore to procure the necessary material to put in two dormer windows in the crews sleeping room, and lathe and plaster the upper rooms of your station, in an open market at the lowest cost obtainable not to exceed $12.65 for the dormer windows and $16.40 for the lathing and plastering.

In 1898 they again improved the station by reshingling the "North addition" and installed a new window in the kitchen. In July of 1900, the station was granted approval to purchase a rather long list of building supplies:

> 1000 feet lumber, common hemlock @ 13.00 per M
> 400 feet lumber, common hemlock dressed @ 14 per M
> 650 feet lumber, No. 2 siding, pine @ 20 per M
> 400 feet lumber No. 2 maple flooring @ 35 per M
> 1000 shingles, cedar, clear butts @ 2 per M

The list also includes curtains and fixtures, door locks, 15 panes of glass, and one "Wedgeway" 14 inch cut lawnmower.

The original 1876 station at Sturgeon Point had the lookout tower located on top of the boat house. On September 24, 1910, District Superintendent Jerome Kiah wrote Keeper Henderson a letter containing the following passage: "In accordance with the request contained in your letter of the 31st ultimo, authority is hereby given you to procure the material necessary for the construction of a new watch house tower and repairs to the outside stairway at your station in the lowest cost obtainable, not to exceed $86.98."

Besides these larger projects there was the accompanying painting and repair of buildings and supplies. During the course of its history at

Sturgeon Point it becomes clear that the Station was continually growing, changing and improving.

Life at Sturgeon Point may have been quiet compared to other stations on the Lakes, but when needed its crew responded as other crews did elsewhere, with amazing professionalism under terrible conditions. Here, as in every other station in the country, the crews employed performed their duties well when called upon. In the meantime, they went about their daily lives and responsibilities as other people. When the weather turned foul the normalcy of their lives was left behind. Instead of closing the shutters and retiring indoors, they reported for duty among the breakers.

Not much remains of the vibrant history of the Sturgeon Point Life-Saving Station . The lighthouse stands as silent now as it did 120 years ago, but if you visit and use your imagination, maybe you can still hear the sound of feet running across the wooden walks of station No. 5 as crew members scrambled for their boats. If you visit late in the fall or early in the spring when the wind is blowing hard out of the north or northeast, perhaps you can hear the whistle of a vessel in distress. If you can use your imagination, it is not hard to see how important the place once was.

Henry J. Cleary, The Showman of the Service

by Frederick Stonehouse
(Volume 2, Issue 1)

July 4, 1891, was a perfect day in Marquette, Michigan. Lake Superior lay flat and calm, although the lake still had a touch of liquid ice just below the surface. The sky above was a perfect blue, unmarred by a single errant cloud. Independence Day was always a day for celebration in the old lake towns and all day long the air was festive with special events and activities. Baseball games, horse races, pie eating contests and Cornish wrestling all competed for public attention.

But one special event stole the show. At precisely 4 o'clock in the afternoon, the Marquette City Band, followed closely by the English Oak Band, both loudly playing lively martial tunes, marched smartly down toward the lower harbor. Streaming along behind was a great crowd of people.

When the procession reached the waterfront, men, women and children flowed onto both ore docks, the merchandise dock, the breakwater and any other perch with a clear view of the water. The local newspaper estimated the throng at more than 5,000 strong. They came from near and far. Most were city residents, proud of their new life-saving crew. After a series of disastrous wrecks in 1886 and 1887 a life-saving station was finally operational in the spring of 1891. Others in the crowd were excursionists visiting the popular "Queen City of Lake Superior." Many were iron miners in town for the celebration from the county's deep rock mines. All were there for one purpose, to watch Keeper Henry J. Cleary and his magnificent U.S. Life-Saving Service crew in action.

Right on time the big white lifeboat shot out of the boathouse, the crew pulling for all they were worth until they reached position midway between the docks. Spinning the boat in a tight circle, the storm warriors received the applause of the crowd.

On signal the crew capsized the boat then righted it. They repeated the maneuver eight times, each time executing all matter of tricks and pranks. After every repetition the crowd cheered more wildly than before. At the end of the final iteration Cleary and his crew took a last bow, then rowed smartly back to the station. Cleary was of course completely dry! As the bog boat rolled, he nimbly scampered just ahead of the water.

Great Lakes crews enacted exhibitions of life-saving skill, similar to the performance the Marquette crew presented on July 4th. And without a doubt, the services' master showman was Marquette's Keeper Cleary.

Born in Port Hope, Michigan in 1862, Cleary sailed commercially on a schooner for several years until he joined the service in 1881 at the age of 19. He was first assigned to Point Aux Barques Life-Saving Station on Lake Huron, just a dozen miles north of his home. Later he served at Port Austin (Grindstone City) and Tawas Life-Saving Stations, also on Lake Huron. His strong leadership qualities and outstanding boat handling skills resulted in his assignment in March, 1885 at the tender age of 23, as keeper of the Deer Park Life-Saving Station, on Lake Superior's infamous "shipwreck coast." This area was considered the most dangerous stretch of the most dangerous lake. He remained at Deer Park until being sent to open the Marquette Life-Saving Station n April 1, 1891.

Cleary was a man of strong physique, enormous endurance and iron nerve. His black handlebar mustache and bright piercing eyes marked him as a man few forgot. When he gave an order it was to be obeyed, instantly! He was however no mindless martinet. Rather he was well respected in the community and his opinion eagerly sought on the issues of the day. Skilled as a carpenter, he built several small houses near the station that he rented to married surfmen.

At Deer Park Life-Saving Station, Cleary led his crew in three demanding rescues. The first occurred on October 23, 1887, when the small steamer *Laketon* was trying to land supplies for a lumber camp near the station. A sudden storm boiled in from the north but instead of

HENRY J. CLEARY

Keeper Henry J. Cleary was the record holder for the fastest breeches buoy drill of all time – an incredible 13 seconds from start to finish! Along with being keeper of Michigan's Marquette Life-Saving Station, he led picked crews of surfmen in performances at major national expositions. The Life-Saving Service selected Keeper Cleary to test the Life-Saving Service's first motor lifeboat. Grand Haven Library photo courtesy of Frederick Stonehouse.

running for shelter to Grand Marais, Michigan, seventeen miles to the west, her captain decided to anchor off the beach and ride it out. Cleary had a better appreciation for the impending disaster and wisely had his crew standing ready. At midnight the steamer's anchor chains broke and the helpless vessel was soon driving hard for the crashing breakers. Without hesitation, Cleary and his men quickly launched the surfboat and brought off the crew without injury. The seas at this time were running so high, he was forced to make the landing stern first, keeping his bow into the cresting combers.

On November 15, 1887, the 218-foot wooden steamer *Starrucca* went hard aground near the station in a screaming gale and blinding snowstorm. Stone-blind from the snow, Cleary only learned of the wreck when two of the ship's crew struggled to the station after landing though the building surf in the yawl. Quickly he assembled his men, dragged the surfboat and wagon over the sand beach to the wreck site, launched and brought off the twenty-one souls remaining aboard. The steamer later broke up completely.

The next night at 7 p.m., during a lull in the gale, the 191-foot steamer *Pacific* went aground on an offshore sandbar near the station. Alerted

Keeper Henry Cleary (upper left in dark uniform) and his first crew of surfmen relaxing on the porch of the Marquette Life-Saving Station, Lake Superior, circa 1891. Marquette Maritime Museum photo courtesy of Frederick Stonehouse.

by the lookout, Cleary and his men immediately went out to the steamer and offered his help, but the steamer's captain refused, saying he could back her off without help. The weather gods however had other plans for the steamer and her crew. By midnight a full gale was howling and the captain now desperately blew his whistle for help. Cleary again led his men to the wreck and using the surfboat, removed the crew of fourteen men and one woman passenger, finally reaching shore at 4 a.m. The crashing waves later broke the *Pacific* into kindling.

Cleary again proved his ability during the dramatic September 21, 1895, rescue of the crew of the steamer *Charles J. Kershaw*. The big steamer went aground in the midst of a roaring gale on a treacherous rock reef just east of Marquette. Braving the terrible storm, thousands of local people watched in awe as Cleary and his surfmen went about their hazardous business. After a risky beach surfboat launch through sharply breaking waves, Cleary deftly plucked nine of the shipwrecked sailors off the rapidly breaking up vessel. During the second launch to remove the four men still aboard, the surfboat was damaged by wreckage surging wildly in the backwash of the waves and several of his men were disabled. Undaunted, he returned to Marquette for the lifeboat and with a crew fleshed out with volunteers in place of the injured men, he launched the big boat and rowed the five miles down to the wreck. Reaching the beleaguered steamer, he nimbly ducked under the stern and the remaining crewman jumped aboard. Within minutes Cleary guided the lifeboat through the breakers to a safe beach landing. This tremendous effort has often been called the greatest Lake Superior rescue of the 1890s.

Regardless of his ability as a USLSS regular keeper, his strongest suit was as a trainer of Life-Saving Service crews. As a mark of how well he was regarded by the Service, he was selected above all other keepers to take a demonstration crew of surfmen to the 1893 Chicago World's Fair. While I know of no specific record supporting this, I would assume that U.S. Life-Saving Service General Superintendent Sumner I. Kimball was closely involved in this decision. Having the trust and confidence of the "beady-eyed little bastard," as Kimball was affectionately known by his crews, was a high honor indeed. Implicit in the assignment was the requirement to train the crew to a razor's edge of proficiency. The crew was not a regular one from a single station, rather it was composed of picked men from different stations across the Life-Saving Service. Although each man was highly competent and selected on his own merit, it was critically important to mold all of them into a perfect team. Every drill the crew demonstrated had to be accomplished to the highest standard possible. Cleary did his job so well that he later took crews to all of the important fairs and expositions: the Trans-Mississippi in Omaha in 1898, the Pan-American Exposition in Buffalo in 1901, the Louisiana Purchase Exposition in St. Louis in 1904, the Jamestown Exposition in Hampton Roads, Virginia, in 1907 and the Alaska-Yukon-Pacific Exposition in Seattle in 1909.

Appearing at such fairs was one of the ways Sumner Kimball used to "sell" the Service to the public. Their importance could not be overemphasized. Cleary not only had to bring the crew to a peak of operational proficiency, but also ensure that the men stayed out of trouble and were model surfmen in all ways. For men brought in from a multitude of isolated stations, being exposed to the idolatry of the crowds and temptations of the big city, it could be a real challenge!

Cleary's men performed in front of tremendous crowds. On the opening day of the Seattle exposition, approximately 25,000 people visited the model station erected on the grounds and watched the crew's drill performance. By the close of the fair five months later, half a million people witnessed the surfmen's performances. In the case of the Seattle show, Cleary did not stay with the crew the entire time. After ensuring they were fully ready to go in all ways, he stayed for two weeks, then turned them over to Keeper Oscar S. Wicklund of the Point Adams Life-Saving Station in Oregon and returned to Marquette.

The number of iterations at the shows was impressive. During the 1907 Jamestown show, the breeches buoy drill was given 146 times and the capsize drill with either lifeboat or surfboat, 562. For the later drill, Cleary was able to hone his crew to the extraordinary time of fourteen seconds, starting from the command "go" with the men in the seats until the moment they were back upright and again at their places. As remarkable as that time was, it was still a second over his St. Louis time of thirteen seconds!

As the years went by, Cleary seemed to defy the ravages of time. During the Seattle show when he was 47, he was still nimble enough to offer his crew a dinner if they were able to get him wet above the knees

Keeper Henry Cleary and surfmen in the Marquette Life-Saving Station's English pulling lifeboat. A surfboat is also on the launchway at right. Marquette Maritime Museum photo courtesy of Frederick Stonehouse.

during the boat drills. Although they tried their best, they never did get the old life-saver wet.

The *Marquette Chronicle* summed up his experiences, "Captain Cleary has without question taken a more active part on world shows than any other man in the city or Michigan. He has perhaps met more of the world's celebrities in the diplomatic, military and marine circles than any other man in the state as his duties as officer in charge of the United States Life-Saving Service exhibit at five great exhibitions have brought him in touch with these notables. Presidents have shaken the captain's hand and taken rides about the lagoons on the grounds of the various shows in the United States life-saving boat. At the Jamestown exposition the Marquette man met naval officers high in command of the world's fleets and no doubt the meeting was a mutual pleasure. At the St. Louis exposition Geronimo, the famous Apache chief, took a fancy to the captain and often rode with him in the government launch. During the Pan American exposition in Buffalo in 1901 he handled the lifeboat that carried President McKinley on his waterways tour the night before the president was assassinated. Just before the murder, Cleary saw the President in the receiving line."

Cleary also had a decided mechanical bent. When the Service decided to test the idea of motorizing lifeboats, it was Cleary with his Marquette Life-Saving Station surfmen that led the way. In 1899, working with an engine designed and built by the city's Lake Shore Iron Company, the crew performed a series of extensive tests and the successful results validated the desirability of motorizing the Service boats.

Captain Cleary died of pneumonia at the station on April 10, 1916. He was fifty-four years old and had been in the Service for thirty-seven years, twenty-five of them as keeper in Marquette. After a large funeral, his body was taken by train to Port Hope on the shores of Lake Huron and interned in the Gore Township Cemetery. He was survived by his wife, one son, two sisters and two brothers (one was George, the keeper at Lake Huron's Bois Blanc Island Life-Saving Station).

Although as old lake sailors said, "he crossed the bar," his legacy lived on, in the minds of the thousands of people who were awed by the faultless drills of his show crews, in the families of the men and women rescued from a grasping lake and in the continued work done by surfmen he trained. Men like John Anderson, later keeper at Two-Heart River and Mackinac Island Stations and Thomas E. Deegan, keeper at Marquette and so many others. Not all of his men made a career of the Life-Saving Service, but all did learn much about facing danger, hard work and courage. Cleary had trained the best.

Shipwrecks On the Jersey Shore: The Henry R. Congdon and Mary F. Kelly

by Margaret Thomas Buchholz

The following is excerpted from *Shipwrecks and Maritime Disasters of the Jersey Shore*, a large-format hardcover released by Down The Shore Publishing in the fall of 2003. The book includes dramatic stories of 60 important wrecks and rescues, an extensive database cataloging the thousands of maritime disasters along the New Jersey Coast, and several hundred illustrations and historical photographs. For more information, visit: www.down-the-shore.com (or write: Down The Shore Publishing, Box 3100, Harvey Cedars, NJ 08008).

Asbury Park's Easter vacationers had come and gone, and the deceptively mild April 1893 weather had townspeople thinking about getting hotels and boarding houses ready for the summer season. But on the 20th they had to batten down for one of those wild, vicious spring northeasters.

A small group of teenage boys went to the beach to watch the storm. They clung to the rail on the north side of the tottering Fifth Avenue pavilion and tried to dodge cascades of spray as they looked to sea through the rain. As the late afternoon light lessened, they saw two three-masted vessels off to the northeast, one much closer to shore than the other. The most seaward of the ships tossed as though she would bounce out of her sticks, and, as they watched, the captain slipped the anchor chain, let out a small triangle of sail on her bowsprit, and attempted to tack off the beach in a southerly direction. She had just enough sea room to maneuver. Swinging perilously close, she cleared the outer bar and was lost to sight in the south. The boys told each other she'd be safe if she could stay off the beach as far as Barnegat Inlet, where the coast makes a swing to the southwest.

The other boat, the *Henry R. Congdon*, was too close to the outer bar for such a tricky operation. If the skipper had cut her anchor chain, she would have been on the bar before he could turn her bow to the south. The boys on the swaying pavilion could see her anchor was dragging, and, with the experience of boys who have watched many a ship strand on the beach, they figured she'd come ashore near Deal, about three-quarters of a mile north. They wanted to walk there on the beach, but four feet of water covered it, and the blowing sand cut their faces sharply enough to raise tiny blotches of blood. So they struggled across the Park Avenue Bridge, hunkering down, trying to protect their faces. When they got to the Deal Lifesaving Station, which had been built twelve years earlier to replace the old Deal Beach station, the men had already left with the apparatus. They soon caught up with the lifesaving crew, and the men were glad of their help. It had been no easy task to drag the cart containing the Lyle gun, signal lights, tripod, breeches buoy, and lines through the gale.

As the rescuers approached the beach, they could see the *Congdon* pounding over the outer bar, giant waves slamming her on the sand with jarring force. It was a question of whether the old schooner would go to pieces there, or be pushed over the bar to the deeper water and washed onto the beach. Leaking in every seam, her spars and rigging slashing in the gale, the vessel slithered over the bar and struck the beach at the foot of the dunes just as the lifesavers arrived. She lay broadside to the beach, giant seas sweeping her decks with, according to one of the boys, "a torrent in which nothing human could survive."

The crew huddled high in the rigging, where they had lashed themselves to escape the huge breakers. The lifesavers lit a cartridge that cast an eerie glow over the scene. By the flickering light, the sailors watched as the men onshore planted the tripod [crotch] at the top of the dune, rigged the breeches buoy, loaded up the Lyle gun, and sent a shot swirling over the ship. After three tries, the line came near enough for a sailor to grab, and he tied it high up on the mast.

It was now dark and the stranded sailors had a choice: to stay lashed in the rigging and pray the mast wouldn't collapse, or to trust the men

The three-masted schooner Henry R. Congdon *wrecked within the area of operation of the Deal Life-Saving Station on the New Jersey coast on April, 1893. A teenage boy who helped the life-saving crew at the scene said the keeper and surfmen predicted the vessel's stranding spot within a hundred feet. Photo use courtesy of Margaret Buchholz and Down the Shore Publishing.*

onshore to carry them safely over the crashing breakers. The up-and-down movement of the ship as each comber slammed it onto the beach guaranteed the ride ashore in the fragile breeches buoy would not be a dry or safe one. But the wreck showed signs of breaking up, and the first sailor thrust his legs into the canvas breeches and gave the signal to haul away.

After what seemed a desperately long time but was only minutes, he landed, exhausted by the daylong fight with the storm and the submersion into the surf as the breeches buoy dipped in and out. The rescued seaman slugged a drink of whiskey and revived. His mates, awaiting their turn in the rigging, saw he was safe and, as one said later, "it nerved us for the perilous adventure." All seven were brought ashore, given a drink, taken to the lifesaving station, fed, and put to bed.

One of the teenagers helping the men recalled later, "It was one of the most brilliant rescues achieved by the Deal Lifesavers. They displayed splendid judgment and absolute accuracy was attained in the handling of lifesaving devices. The spot on the beach where the vessel would strand had been judged within a hundred feet."

By morning, the wind had shifted to the north, flattening the sea. The *Henry R. Congdon* was now a battered hulk high and dry on the beach, where it stayed for most of the summer. Her hull was eventually turned into a real estate office, but it went to pieces in a later storm.

By August 23 Asbury Park's summer season was peaking. The Columbia and Brunswick hotels were fully booked; crowds jostled each

According to historian Ralph Shanks and architectural historian Wick York in their book The United States Life-Saving Service: Heroes, Rescues and Architecture of the Early Coast Guard, *the Deal Life-Saving Station at Asbury Park, New Jersey, was one of the most decorative stations ever built by the service. Photo use courtesy of Ralph Shanks and* The United States Life-Saving Service: Heroes, Rescues and Architecture of the Early Coast Guard.

other as they strolled along the boardwalk. The ladies' long white skirts moved in the breeze, and gentlemen in high collars tipped their bowlers to pretty young women. All were glad that James Bradley, the town's developer, had finished the bicycle path, making the boardwalk less hazardous for pedestrians. The shimmering sea lapped placidly on the sand, sails scudded along the horizon, and vacationers protected themselves from the suddenly oppressive heat under large black umbrellas. The light had a mystical, evanescent quality.

In the evening the soft, southeast breeze picked up, the barometer started to fall, and by 10 o'clock a full gale with pelting rain had closed the town's amusement park and casino and driven vacationers indoors. By 2 o'clock in the morning, a hurricane force wind buffeted the town. At dawn, Clark Hurley, one of Asbury Park's town watchmen, spotted a battered hulk through the driving sheets of rain. He thought a barge had broken loose, but as he watched it tumble closer to shore, he realized it was a dismasted schooner. The boat washed past the fishing pier and headed straight for the Fifth Avenue pavilion. Hurley saw it graze the pavilion and bury its nose in the sand. He saw no signs of life onboard.

Christopher Grattan, captain of the two-masted, 60-ton schooner *Mary F. Kelly* out of Brooklyn, had been fishing for several days when he dropped anchor off Manasquan that day at dusk. He and his crew of 10 had no way of knowing a hurricane was churning up the coast. When the fishermen realized that the weather was turning dangerous, they mustered on deck in their oilcloth suits, checked the lines, and battened down the hatches. But the powerful wind and the shock of successive heavy seas snapped the anchor cable, and the little vessel began to drive with the current toward the beach. The steward decided he was safer below and stayed in his cabin.

The captain made several attempts to set the sails, with the hope of working the schooner offshore, but the howling wind shredded the canvas. The fishermen now contemplated the gloomy prospect of crossing the terrifying breakers between their helpless craft and shore. Their only hope was that they might hold on until the shallow-draft schooner stranded well up on the beach. Captain Grattan stayed at the wheel and kept as good control as possible of the bucking craft, but just as she crossed the breakers a giant wave overwhelmed the boat. It burst over the deck, cracked the mast, and swept the captain, his mate, and one seaman overboard. Their bodies were recovered later, miles to the north.

Hurley's first impulse was to run to the lifesaving station and give the alarm, but the most direct route along the beach was blocked by the heavy surf and high tide, which submerged the narrow strip of sand separating Deal Lake from the ocean. Instead, he gave a general alarm that a vessel was coming ashore.

J.E. Wortman, an Asbury Park resident, had gone to the beach early that morning. Wortman was one of those longtime shore residents who could smell trouble, and in a storm like this it was likely a ship would be in distress. As soon as he examined the *Kelly's* position, he was convinced that only the lifesaving apparatus could rescue the sailors. Spectators swarmed over the beach, and he called on some men he knew to follow him. They struggled through warm, waist-deep water along the narrow strip of beach to the Deal Lifesaving Station.

Even though it was eight days before the station's official opening for the season, Keeper Lambert Edwards had been patrolling the beach most of the night. He returned from the north just as Wortman reached the station with news of the wreck to the south. Edwards asked Wortman to run for reinforcements, and sent a surfman named Slocum to the nearest hotel for a horse to haul the beach cart. Water surrounded the station's stable, and the horse kept there balked at going into the surf. But Slocum soon returned with a more agreeable horse, and Wortman with volunteers. The rising tide beat against the boathouse doors, but the men forced them open and wheeled the apparatus cart out to the horse on the lee side of the station. But the water had risen so high that they had to use a roundabout, inland route to get to the *Kelly*.

Meanwhile, over a thousand curiosity seekers crowded up and down the boardwalk. They watched with horror as the schooner's crew tried to hold on to the wallowing craft, in one moment riding high on the crest of a wave and the next plunging beneath a boiling breaker.

It took nearly an hour from the time Keeper Edwards learned about the *Kelly* to get on the beach opposite the wreck, which now lay with her bow to the north. The tide had carried her to within 40 or 50 feet of the small pavilion jutting out from the boardwalk. There she lay with her masts fallen. Six of the crew had already been rescued; bystanders had hauled two men ashore with ropes, while the other crewmembers had crawled to the beach along a fallen spar. A seventh survivor, still onboard, appeared to be confused and was about to leap into the surf when one of the lifesavers threw him a heaving-stick (a stick with a line attached for rescues close to shore). The sailor fastened the line to his body, and the lifesavers pulled him onto solid ground.

The survivors were taken to the Hotel Columbia, where the proprietor fed them and they got some rest. Keeper Edwards brought clothing from the station, and by late afternoon the rescued crew was on the train for New York, with money in their pockets donated by the citizens of Asbury Park.

When the storm tide receded, Keeper Edwards boarded the schooner and found her masts cut off at the deck, the bowsprit carried away at the knightheads, the rudderhead twisted off, the rail and bulwarks crushed in, and the partitions and bulkheads within the hull broken down and scattered. The steward was still in his cabin, his broken body askew and his skull crushed.

The Lifesaving Service's investigating officer wrote in his official report: "It is marvelous how any members of the schooner's company held on to the wreck through the terrible breakers. Had the weather been cold and the spray freezing, it is likely that not one of them would have survived. The four men who were lost met their unhappy fate on the outer bar at about the time the vessel was first seen from the shore. No earthly power could have saved them."

Surfman Attacked and Robbed On Patrol

by John J. Galluzzo
(Volume 2, Issue 3)

Every night for ten months of the year, turn-of-the-century surfmen employed by the U.S. Life-Saving Service patrolled the nation's shorelines, vigilantly watching for any sign of ships in distress. Through any kind of weather, be it driving April rain, blinding January snow, or muggy August heat, they covered an average of five miles per four-hour patrol. Most nights passed uneventfully; others brought surprises.

Charles Jennings, who later became the keeper of the Lovell's Island Range Lights, spent time as a young man as a surfman at Cahoon's Hollow LSS Station on Cape Cod. One night, word reached the station that a local farmer's bull had escaped and was probably out on the beach.

While out on patrol that night, almost walking in a trance from the sheer monotony, Jennings caught movement out of the corner of his eye, a large form careening over the dunes toward him. He ran for his life towards the water, but felt a whack on the back of his legs just before he reached the surf. Terrified and confused, he dove to the ground, and looked around at his attacker- a rolling, wind-driven fish barrel.

He stood up, brushed himself off, looked around to see if there were any witnesses, and then completed his patrol.

When he returned to the station, he found out that the bull had been captured on the other side of the Cape. Then and there, he decided to never mention to any of his fellow surfmen that he had been scared out of his wits by a rolling barrel.

Surfman Clarence Smith of the Gurnet Station in Plymouth went out on patrol, as usual, the night of March 23, 1894, but did not return by the expected time. Worried about his surfman, the keeper of the station walked the patrol to find him. After the keeper had walked the entire patrol, out and back, he returned to the station to find Smith standing in the front yard, perfectly safe from harm.

When asked where he had been, Surfman Smith replied, "I will tell you the truth, I have been away with a woman, but I should not have done it if it had not been a bright moonlight (sic) night." The keeper fired him on the spot.

Even the lifesavers in Hull had to expect the unexpected. Returning from patrols to Pemberton Point in January of 1898, Joshua James' surfmen began to tell this tale: "Almost every night during the 'dog watch,' the lifesavers while on patrol near Battery Heights, one of the loneliest parts of the town, meet a strange woman, unknown to them, who walks beside them for a few moments without speaking, then suddenly disappears. Several of the patrolmen have met her and her strange conduct is creating considerable comment." (Hull Beacon).

After two weeks, the visitations stopped. Strangely, though, the spot described by the lifesavers, at the base of the sheer hill in front of the Jacobs School, is the same spot from which Melanie Lanier allegedly launched her dory the night she rowed out to save her Confederate prisoner husband Samuel who was being held at Fort Warren on George's Island during the Civil War. The lifesavers' encounters possibly have been some of the first recorded incidents in connection with the legendary "Lady in Black."

The lifesavers expected on any given night to have to battle Mother Nature; they never expected to have to wrestle with human nature. Due to the reputation that came with their uniforms, the surfmen were held in high respect by the citizenry for, after all, they risked their lives on a regular basis to save others. The last thing a surfman would be thinking about on patrol was being assaulted. That is, until one early March night in 1900.

On Friday night, March 1 of that year, Surfman Fernando Bearse of the Point Allerton Life-Saving Station drew the long patrol, eastward out of the station to Point Allerton, and then southward to a keypost at A St. He had walked the patrol many times since arriving in Hull in 1897 and knew every inch of his route.

Surfman Fernando F. Bearse, third from left, mourns at the funeral of Keeper Joshua James of the Point Allerton Life-Saving Station, Hull, Massachusetts. United States Coast Guard photo.

That afternoon he had withdrawn $172 from his bank account in Hingham. He and his wife, the former Helen Litchfield of Hull, had been planning to visit his family in Chatham and get away for a day or two.

The first half of his patrol passed uneventfully. Stepping into the small halfway shed that housed the keypost, he punched his patrol clock and commenced building a fire to warm himself for the trip back.

When he was ready to go, he stepped out of the hut and locked it. Before he could take another step, an assailant blind-sided him in the darkness, knocking him to the sand. Completely surprised, Bearse found himself wrestling for his life on the beach, but soon managed to gain the upper hand and escape.

He ran off the beach and across the tracks. But there, on the other side, two more men stood waiting for him. The first, covered in sand, joined the others in pinning him to the ground, demanding that he turn over his money. Outnumbered, and fearing for his life, he acceded to their demands. The attackers then ran off into the darkness, leaving the battered lifesaver to stumble home.

When he returned to the station, covered in sand, he told Captain James his tale. He described the three men as "stalwart fellows," one of whom wore a full thick beard.

For ten years the Point Allerton lifesavers had been walking the same patrols, ten months a year, seven nights a week, up to sixteen hours a night, and not once had anyone been attacked. Yet the one night that a lifesaver happened to be carrying a large sum of money on him, about three months' salary, he was assaulted and robbed. His assailants knew where and when to find him, and knew that A St. in wintertime would consist of nothing but boarded up summer homes and complete and utter darkness and solitude. Whether they received inside information from a contact in the bank, or simply overheard that he had the money, they knew he would have it on him. This had to be a premeditated assault.

Word soon spread through the wintertime community to watch out for three strangers, one with a beard. Shopkeepers became suspicious of anybody flashing large bills, tens and twenties. None of the wealthy summer residents had arrived for the season just yet, so no one had any reason to spread that kind of wealth around.

Hull had always been proud of her lifesaving reputation. Between 1848 and 1898, townsfolk had earned 275 medals for bravery, not even counting the deeds of the U.S.L.S.S. surfmen. When you spoke of Hull, you spoke of lifesaving. So when Bearse was attacked, the whole community felt the shock and closed ranks around him.

Fernando Bearse never did identify his attackers. However, four nights later, while paired up on patrol with Surfman Francis B. Mitchell, he did find a surprise. Stepping into the keypost shed a A St. on Tuesday night, Mitchell stooped to light a fire but was startled by a cry from Bearse.

It was a cry of joy.

There, on the bench, wrapped in an elastic, lay a large wad of bills. When counted, it totaled $130. It was not quite what he had started with, but it was close enough. Maybe he and his wife would get that vacation after all.

Lawrence O. Lawson: An Extraordinary Keeper

by Dennis L. Noble
(Volume 6, Issue 1)

A desired trait in keepers of the U.S. Life-Saving Service was leadership. One of the best examples of the embodiment of this trait was Lawrence Oscar Lawson of the Evanston, Illinois, station. Lawson was born September 11, 1842 at Kalmar, Sweden. At the age of eighteen he went to sea. He traveled to New York in 1861 and continued his profession of sailor.[1]

By 1864, Lawson made his way to Chicago, where he worked as a fisherman and sailed on lake ships. Five years later he moved to Evanston and soon thereafter Ludington, Michigan, only to return to Evanston in 1878. With his large amount of sea time, Lawson was a natural for the position of keeper at the Evanston station and received the appointment in 1880. He remained in this position for close to twenty-three years.

In 1902, a local newspaper commented that Lawson, at the age of sixty, was still able to undertake the "daily boat drill and manipulates the heavy beach apparatus." By the next year, however, failing vision caused his "retirement." (Retirement from the Life-Saving Service oftentimes meant that a person could no longer pass the required physical and had to leave the organization without retirement pay or other benefits). Lawson was responsible during his career for the "rescue of over 500 persons from the stormy waters of Lake Michigan." Keeper Lawrence O. Lawson died on October 29, 1912.

While serving honorably for a long period of time, Lawson's career at first glance does not seem far different from many other long-service keepers. What makes Keeper Lawson different is the make-up of his crew.

Keeper Lawrence O. Lawson and his Evanston, Illinois, student crew five years after the rescue of the Calumet. *The age difference between the keeper and crew is evident. In later years, most writers of the area commented upon the length of Lawson's beard. Beloved by his men, Lawson only left his position with the Life-Saving Service when his eyesight began to fail him. United States Coast Guard photo.*

The Evanston station was located on the grounds of Northwestern University. In 1871 a boat was given to the university to be manned by the school's students. A red-brick station was built in 1876. "At the annual graduation exercises, the life-saving boat was handed down by the seniors to the junior class and a new captain was chosen." Eventually, it was thought there needed to be an experienced seaman to "make seamen of the eager but inexperienced students." Lawson, with years of sea experience, received the call.

One can only imagine how an old salt would have felt about whipping a group of young college students into shape in order to survive the dangers of maritime rescue. Indeed, "fears were expressed that an outsider would not be able to get the cooperation of the student crew and that the appointment of Captain Lawson would be the first step toward the severance of relations between the university and the life-saving station." Keeper Lawson surprised everyone. Within a short period of time, Lawson's skills "succeeded in winning the loyalty of the crew." George H. Tomlinson, a former crewmember, would later recall, "The most eventful period of the station's history began with the appointment of Captain Lawson...as keeper of the station. He... won the love and respect of all who entered the university in that time. As a member of one of the student crews who served under him, I can attest to his courage, ability and fineness of character - a rare soul such as does not often come into one's life."

Tomlinson wrote, "No one who has not had the privilege of waking [Lawson] in the middle of the night to report some emergency could envision him coming out of his bedroom into the hall with his long white nightgown and his long graying beard, with one hand searching his ribs, either for the answer or to help him awaken, and the other hand twisting his beard back and forth."

Lawson apparently never lost his patience, even when things were a little different at Evanston than at other units of the service. In 1900, for example, the Chicago Tribune reported that Lawson feared his surfmen were not keeping their minds strictly on their duties because "every afternoon, before and after drill, the members are surrounded by bevies of young women talking to the lifesavers. Even when it is time for their favorites to go on patrol duty the young women do not depart, but turn their attention to the reserve men."[2]

Many years later, one of Keeper Lawson's sons would relate that in the "summer, when the boys wore white suits, we got quite a few calls from people around Calvary cemetery. They thought they were seeing ghosts."

William E. McLennan, another former member of the Evanston crew, remarked that Lawson "has never been known to give up the most forlorn hope so long as human lives were in danger." This statement was more than proved on Thanksgiving Day 1889.

The 1,500-ton steamer *Calumet* ran afoul of one of Lake Michigan's late fall storms. Earlier, the ship had hit a submerged anchor in the Detroit River and had sprung a leak, and the steam pumps keeping the ship afloat finally gave out. The leak, combined with the storm, spelled the end of the ship. To save his crew of seventeen, the captain ran his vessel aground and ordered the valves in the bottom of the vessel opened to flood the hold and prevent the ship from going to pieces in the pounding waves.[3]

The *Calumet* grounded at 10:30 P.M. and some time passed before a local resident discovered the wreck and wired the Evanston station, about twelve miles away. Keeper Lawson received the telegram shortly after midnight and immediately checked with the local railroad station. A freight train to transport his boat and beach cart would not be available until 7:30 A.M., but a passenger train could be stopped soon to carry his crew to the site. Lawson next ran through the snow to a livery stable and rented teams of horses to pull the boat, beach equipment and some of the crew by road, while he and the remainder went by train to survey the situation and be ready to act when the team arrived.

The *Calumet* lay submerged almost to her main deck with waves breaking over her, near 70-to-80 foot brush covered bluffs. Once the horse-drawn beach apparatus arrived, at about 7 A.M., Keeper Lawson had the beach apparatus rigged. After two unsuccessful shots, he realized that the wreck lay well beyond the 600-yard range of the lines. If the sailors were to be saved, Lawson's last recourse was the boat, despite the heavy surf that lashed the foot of the bluff. Aided by about fifty soldiers from nearby Fort Sheridan, and some civilians, the lifesavers cut brush and wrestled the boat down the bluff to the beach.

Working waist-deep in the icy water, the soldiers and civilians managed to get the boat into position, slightly windward of the wreck and facing lakeward. Then, as the next wave lifted the boat, they gave a mighty push, while the lifesavers sprang to their places at the oars. An immense breaker struck as the boat crossed the inner bar, almost throwing Lawson overboard from his position at the stern sweep oar and, before he could recover himself, a second wave dashed over the boat and filled it to the thwarts. Lawson ordered a surfman to ply the bailing bucket, while the five other lifesavers pulled at their oars to control the almost unmanageable boat until it was freed of water and beyond the heaviest line of surf. By this time, the strong current had driven the boat far to the leeward, giving them a long and hard pull directly into the gale.

LAWRENCE O. LAWSON

Lawson stood in the stern, facing the full brunt of the storm and exhorting his crew. The freezing temperature encased the crew's clothing, oars, and oarlocks with a sheet of ice. A former crewman on the rescue would later say, "I really believed we were all going to our death. Still I knew the captain and I knew the other boys...I never knew exactly how we reached the steamer, but I will never forget the welcome those poor devils of sailors gave us. We took a half dozen of them aboard the boat, and then set out on our return trip. I thought the following wave would swamp us, but as each cloud of spray went by I could see the Captain standing at his post, his long beard matted with ice, but his voice as calm as if we were on a drill."

Once six passengers had been lowered by rope - all the boat could carry - the lifesavers bent to their oars and rowed shoreward. The awaiting soldiers and civilians rushed them to a blazing bonfire and gave them hot coffee. Lawson once again ordered his crew out into the gale. "The second trip was like the first, except that it was harder, for we were cold and worn out, but we made it to safety. When the time came for the third trip, some of the boys felt mighty like giving up, and the soldiers and the bystanders told us we had done enough. Still, we went without a murmur when the Captain ordered us out, and somehow we got through safely." All eighteen sailors on the *Calumet* were safely brought ashore.

By the time that they reached shore on their last trip, the lifesavers were in almost as bad a plight as the men they had saved, being so numb they could scarcely walk. For their outstanding actions on this cold, stormy night in November the entire crew of the Evanston station received the Gold Life Saving Medal. How the service judged the performance of Keeper Lawson and his crew is shown by this simple statistic: between 1876 and 1908 there were only ten cases where the entire crew of a U.S. Life-Saving Service station received the Gold Life Saving Medal.

Former crewman William E. McClennan said it best: "Without [Keeper Lawrence O. Lawson] as a leader through almost a quarter of a century, the Evanston life-saving crew could hardly have won for itself much more than average fame."

"A Hard Day On All of Us": Indian River Inlet Station and the Wreck of the Anna Murray

by Bob Trapani, Jr.
(Volume 7, Issue 4)

On the morning of February 17, 1902, as a terrible snowstorm blew hard from the northeast, Calvin W. Haith, surfman No. 4, scaled the steps leading to the frigid cupola of Indian River Inlet (DE) Life-Saving Station. From his perch high atop the station, Surfman Haith was tasked with keeping a careful watch seaward for ships that might founder in the raging waters of the Atlantic Ocean.

Within a couple of hours the fury of the tempest made it nearly impossible for Surfman Haith to see but a mere hundred or so yards eastward of the life-saving station. It was at this time that keeper Washington A. Vickers informed his crew that the day-watch from the safe confines of the cupola would be immediately suspended and shifted out into the realm of the gale where a dangerous ice-laden, surf-swept beach awaited.

Without hesitation, Calvin Haith and Thomas Dukes, surfman No. 3, donned their foul-weather gear, absorbed the final moments of warmth afforded by the snug station and then commenced a beach patrol by walking side by side towards a seething ocean. Once at water's edge, Haith set out north towards the Rehoboth Beach (Delaware) Life-Saving Station and Dukes southward to the keybox at Indian River Inlet.

At about 9:30 a.m., nearly an hour and a half into Surfman Duke's dreadful march, the storm temporarily abated sufficiently enough for him to espy a peculiar, water-locked object that he estimated to be one mile south of the ice-strewn Indian River Inlet. Surfman Dukes immediately decided to return to the station and alert keeper Vickers of the sighting, knowing all the while that his arduous walk back through the frozen mire from which he had come must be done in the most urgent of manners. Dukes eventually burst through the back door of the station, and though gasping for air in his exhaustion, quickly recounted his findings to Vickers and the remainder of the crew.

The station's daily log recounts the frightful tempest as Keeper Vickers penned, "it had been snowing and blowing a hurricane since midnight - impossible to see but a short distance at anytime. He (Surfman Dukes) returned to the station and he reported the situation to me - the keeper, at the same time he said the inlet was all blocked up with ice which had come in from the Delaware."

Keeper Vickers, upon hearing Surfman Duke's alarming report, realized that his crew had little to no chance of successfully landing the beach apparatus on the opposite side of the ice-laden inlet, so he decided to place a telephone call to keeper John H. Long of the Fenwick Island (DE) Life-Saving Station. Vickers penned the following remarks in the station's daily log about his decision to phone for assistance, saying, "I telephoned to Keeper Long at Fenwick Island Station - asked him if he could come up the beach with his crew and team and bring the gear from the halfway house. I stated the trouble we were in and did not know that we would be able to get [our gear] across. His reply was that he would and that I could depend on him getting there as soon as possible."

Springing into action, the Indian River Inlet life-savers gathered their gear and readied to hitch the team for a laborious, frozen pull of one mile southward to the banks of the inlet. As the surfmen slid open the heavy wood doors of the boat room, the raging blizzard sent swirls of snow throughout the first floor of the 1876 station. Undaunted, the crew rolled their equipment down the ramp and into the teeth of the wintry tempest. Following a strenuous trek to the inlet, the crew quickly realized why Keeper Vickers was concerned about their ability to cross the treacherous waterway, as blocks of tumbled and jagged ice floes and a racing current beneath the crystal chaos were collectively too much to fight against. Vickers describes the icy scene, stating, "when we reached the inlet, we found it was impossible to get the team or gear across and would be all that we could do to get ourselves across by using a small boat that we might haul over and between blocks of ice."

Keeper Washington Vickers served at the Indian River Inlet (DE) Life-Saving Station from 1883-1910, and led the rescue of the four-masted schooner Anna Murray *in 1902.*
Photo courtesy of Marjorie Wellborn.

Knowing the Fenwick Island crew was bringing the beach apparatus from the halfway house to the south, Washington Vickers instructed his surfmen to carry only a small line-heaving stick, boat hook, pickax, breeches buoy and a shovel in the small boat. The crew left the remainder of their equipment behind with the team of horses on the northern banks of the Indian River Inlet. After a prodigious effort of pushing and pulling their boat over and through a maze of treacherous ice, the life-savers successfully reached the other side of the beach. Despite a safe crossing of the inlet, the effort did nothing to lessen the hardships of the crew as they discovered the flats were covered for a half-mile with blocks of pancaked ice. Refusing to despair, Keeper Vickers encouraged his crew and pressed forward in resolute fashion, all the while continuing to battle the raging elements, bitter cold and exhaustion.

Two fatigue-filled hours later, around 11:30 a.m., the life-savers arrived near the site of the stricken vessel, which proved to be the four-masted schooner *Anna Murray*. Vickers assessed the dire situation, saying, "she lay about 75 yards from the beach, listed offshore pounding and grinding heavy with an awful sea." Before long, the spunky crew from the Fenwick Island Life-Saving Station reached the wreck as well, having obtained the beach apparatus from the halfway house as requested. Keeper Long then joined Keeper Vickers in a discussion as to what would be the most timely and effective means of rescuing the shipwrecked mariners amidst the blizzard.

In the meantime, the horrific conditions being spawned by the storm grew worse with each passing hour. The combination of a rising tide and powerful winds began to send devastating storm surge awash over the ice-laden beach, with some spots being inundated some six to eight feet in depth. All the while, the foundering *Anna Murray* was being hammered mercilessly by such frightening seas that spray and ice were sent flying upwards half-mast high.

Though held prisoner within Old Man Winter's icy grip, the crew aboard *Anna Murray* appeared to be in fair condition, owing their well being primarily to the strength of a new and well-constructed schooner. Throughout their terrifying ordeal, the captain and his crew watched anxiously as the life-savers scurried to set up rescue operations on the forsaken beach. Despite the deafening noise created by the storm's thunderous waves and howling winds, the captain of the schooner was able to consistently communicate with the surfmen by using a megaphone. Information such as the condition of *Anna Murray* and that of her crew was periodically relayed to shore by the captain's voice enhancement. Keeper Vickers acknowledged the captain by signaling back to the mariners that life-saving gear would soon be in place and deployed to take them off the shipwreck.

Before long a 2-ounce charge of black powder propelled a 17-pound projectile from the Lyle Gun and sent it hurtling through the blizzard towards *Anna Murray*. The aim of the Indian River life-savers was true as the shot landed over the vessel, allowing the sailors aboard the ship to haul off the whip which was fastened to the highest point on the mast as instructed. Yet despite the knowledge of a secure line and the fact that the tempest threatened their lives at every turn, the crew of *Anna Murray* remained apprehensive about entrusting their fate to a breeches buoy being pulled over raging seas. Knowing time was of the essence, Keeper Vickers decided he could not wait for the crew to muster the courage to utilize the life-saving breeches buoy. Instead, he instilled a confidence within the stricken crew for the rescue apparatus by personally making the first trip from shore off to the wreck. Later,

Keeper Vickers would comment about his decision of bravery, saying, "my going off seemed to give them confidence in the buoy."

In anticipation of being rescued, the crew had packed all their personal belongings and proved more than ready to abandon the shipwreck as Keeper Vickers boarded the ship. Under the watchful eye of Vickers, the crew of ten men and their personal affects were systematically and safely landed on the beach one by one. In all, the life-savers from Indian River Inlet and Fenwick Island utilized the breeches buoy for 25 separate trips to and from the ship, all without incident despite the presence of hurricane force winds and blinding snow.

Though the sailors were safely brought ashore, their hardships were only partially over. The fact that the location of *Anna Murray* was 2.5 miles south of the Indian River Life-Saving Station presented another arduous ordeal to the fatigued surfmen and rescued mariners. Fighting severe exhaustion and hypothermia, the men set out on a 1.5-mile trek north over the ice-strewn beaches of quicksand just to reach the inlet where they previously left some of their equipment and boat.

By the time the crew arrived at the Indian River Inlet, high tide flooded the cut of the waterway due to the packed ice that prevented the raging current from encountering an even flow. Blocks of ice were also thrust up onto the banks of the inlet, and in many cases, carried on the flats of the beach. Keeper Vickers described this awful scene, stating, "we had to wade the crew over the flats, through the slush and water and over the blocks of ice for a half-mile to reach the boat. We made three trips in getting the crew across the inlet, but did it all successfully."

Once the surfmen led the shipwrecked sailors across the inlet, the entire party still faced a frozen tramp of one mile further in distance to reach the Indian River Life-Saving Station. Finally, by 5:00 o'clock in the evening the life-savers and the crew of *Anna Murray* reached the station. The sailors were promptly provided dry clothes, made comfortable and given warm food and drink. The appreciative captain and crew of *Anna Murray* profusely thanked Keeper Washington A. Vickers and his brave surfmen time and again for their efforts to rescue them from a certain doom had not Surfman Dukes spotted their ship trapped within the death-grip of a sandy shoal. The mariners also stated that there is "no service that equals the Life-Saving Service." Unfortunately the schooner itself could not be saved. After two days of salvage work, the wreckers and the ship's owner determined that they could not save the vessel. Hence, a decision was made to strip everything movable from the deck and hull and to leave the lifeless hulk to its demise at the merciless hands of the sea.

The shipwreck *Anna Murray* went down in the annals of Indian River Inlet Life-Saving Station's history as one of the finest examples of valor and dedication exhibited by its crews. In his usual modest fashion, Keeper Vickers did not seek special attention for the heroics of his crew and him. In fact, he simply summed up the event in the station's daily log by saying, "this has been a hard day on all of us. I think everything has been managed as well as could have been under the circumstances."

Gold Medals On the Jersey Shore

by Margaret Thomas Buchholz
(Volume 7, Issue 4)

The following is excerpted from the book *New Jersey Shipwrecks: 350 Years in the Graveyard of the Atlantic* by Margaret Thomas Buchholz, released by Down The Shore Publishing. The large-format hardcover includes dramatic accounts of 60 major wrecks and rescues, a listing of hundreds of other maritime disasters along the New Jersey Coast, and 142 illustrations and historical photographs. For more information, visit: www.down-the-shore.com (or write: Down The Shore Publishing, Box 3100, Harvey Cedars, NJ 08008).

Four Crewmen Saved From Abiel Abbott, Five Drowned

On January 20, 1903, a northeaster blasted the Jersey Shore with freezing rain and snow, searing wind and high seas. It proved too much for the 28-year-old Abiel Abbott, sailing from the Turks and Caicos to New York, and the bark stranded on the bar off what is now Eighth Street in Ship Bottom, 500 yards from the beach. At 8:15 pm a surfman on patrol discovered the bark aground. Isaac Truex, keeper of the Ship Bottom Lifesaving Station, and his men shouldered the lines and dragged the cedar-planked surfboat to the beach. But to launch it in the pitch darkness would have been suicide, so Truex opted to use the Lyle gun. He and his men fired four lines in the next several hours, but the crew, high in the rigging, could not reach any of them.

Truex telephoned for help and Keeper Alexander Falkinburg brought his crew from Harvey Cedars and Keeper George Mathis and his men

The Ship Bottom Life-Saving Station crew stands before their station. Photo courtesy of Down the Shore Publishing.

came up from the Long Beach station. But all they could do was stand by until daylight.

At first light, they heard cries for help and saw the boat was breaking up, with men still tangled in the rigging. They rowed the surfboat through the breakers, but they could get within only 50 yards of the Abbott before having to turn back: The boat had taken on so much water they were barely able to keep it afloat. On the second try, broken and jagged wreckage threatened them with each pull of the oars - it was an obstacle course they couldn't navigate, and they were beaten back to shore. The men were exhausted and their oilskins had frozen to their boots. "We felt like icicles," Walter Pharo later said. "We cracked whenever we moved. It was the worst night I ever put in on the beach."

While the lifesavers were trying to reach the Abbott, the mizzenmast collapsed and three men drowned. Captain Isaac B. Hawkins, the bark's 70-year-old master, and four of his crew - Otto Berg, James Burns,

Frank Levin, and James Butler - held onto the deckhouse that had broken off and jammed onto the bar. The captain was bleeding from the head, and he and his men were fighting a losing battle with the freezing water when Truex and his lifesavers went into the surf for the third try. This time they edged their boat alongside the deckhouse and helped the five men into the surfboat. It was 9 am when they got them back to the station. One man was unconscious, and Sprague and his men worked on him for almost an hour but couldn't resuscitate him. At the hearing following the wreck, Captain Hawkins testified that he had believed it was impossible for the lifesavers to get to them. "That they succeeded in doing so was a miracle," he said.

Pieces of the 136-foot Abiel Abbott were strewn all over the beach. A patrolman found First Mate Joseph H. Pearce's body the next day;

Surfman V.C. Conklin (and friend) of the Ship Bottom Life-Saving Station display his Gold Life-Saving Medal. Photo courtesy of Down the Shore Publishing.

his kit bag was found nearby and contained many letters from his wife and children. The bodies of seamen Henry Carter, Timothy Brandt, and Steward Charles Palmer did not wash up until a week later.

Lieutenant Barthold, chief inspector of the Life-Saving Service, said that the men remained on the beach the entire night and acted heroically in their efforts to get to the stranded vessel. In recognition of their heroic conduct, Congress awarded gold lifesaving medals to Keeper Truex and Surfmen J. Horace Cranmer, James Cranmer, Walter Pharo, Barton Pharo, Abraham B. Salmons, and C. V. Conklin from the Ship Bottom station. Keeper George Mathis and surfmen W. E. Pharo and M. D. Kelly of the Long Beach station, who helped man the surfboat, also received the Life-Saving Service's highest award. This Congressional medal was awarded only when the rescuer risked losing his life. It was not awarded very often, since Congress had decreed that possible loss of life went with the job.

Pound Fishermen Aid Squan Beach Lifesavers

Pound fishing was a well-established industry from Long Branch south to Ocean City by 1900. The fishery was started a generation earlier by Scandinavians who had migrated south from Brooklyn, and it went hand-in-hand with the development of the coastal railway system that transported the fish to market. A fish pound "impounded" the catch in a complex system of nets attached to 90-foot poles embedded in the ocean floor a mile or two offshore. A line ran from the beach to a pole 200 yards out, and the fishermen pulled their skiffs out hand over hand, stern first, then turned the boat around and rowed to the pound (engines were used after 1915). The lapstrake cedar skiffs were so heavy when loaded that a team of horses (and later tractors) had to haul them back to the beach.

On June 13, 1903, a strong southerly wind and a heavy ground swell built a high surf, which in Manasquan was breaking all the way from the bar to the beach. Despite the conditions, a few of the more daring (or perhaps foolhardy) pound fishermen launched their 33-foot boats. Early in the morning, one crew - Captain John K. Andersen, Harry Andersen and five others - skidded their boat down to the surf and pushed off, heading to the fish pound 2 miles out. About noon they started back, their skiff heavily loaded. Moments later, just beyond the bar, a large wave capsized the boat and threw the fishermen into the water. They grabbed the overturned boat and held on.

Charlie Bowker, another fisherman, was watching from the beach. He immediately ran to a small fishing skiff and dragged it to the water. As he was unsuccessfully trying to talk someone into coming with him, Keeper Robert Longstreet of the Squan Beach station arrived on the beach. Since it was the inactive season there was no crew on duty at the station and no time to look for volunteers. Without hesitation, the two men jumped in and stroked toward the endangered fishermen.

Rowing the boat through the surf was a difficult and dangerous task for only two oarsmen. They had to fight an adverse wind, heavy seas, and a strong onshore current. Only one man could row because the other had to bail constantly just to keep ahead of the waves breaking over them. "By persistent and skillful effort," said the life-saving report submitted later, Longstreet and Bowker worked the skiff over to the capsized boat, now awash in a crosscurrent of breaking waves. The waves broke over her so furiously that five of the men were washed off - fortunately in the direction of shore. Captain Andersen and the only remaining fisherman, Alfred Carlsen, held on. According to the report, "Captain Andersen might have been able to save himself, but he gallantly refused to abandon the other man, who could not swim. He remained by him, swimming in the lee of the boat ready to sustain him in case he should lose his hold."

Longstreet got close enough so that Andersen could get a hold on the stern. But just as the captain started to pull himself up, a wave loosened the grip of the hapless non-swimmer. At this critical moment, Andersen kept his wits about him and grabbed his buddy by the arm while Longstreet, leaning out of the skiff, seized Andersen and held him until the breaker had passed. It happened faster than it takes to tell. Both men were pulled onboard, and Longstreet and Bowker maneuvered the boat quickly back to shore.

In the meantime, only four of the five men who had washed from the capsized boat, including Harry Andersen, had reached the beach: The fifth, a weak swimmer, disappeared under the water just before they got ashore. Reacting quickly, Harry Andersen tied a line around his waist and plunged back into the breakers. He found his friend floating about 40 feet from shore, and he put his arms under his shoulders and supported him while three men quickly hauled them to the beach. By that time, Keeper Longstreet had arrived onshore, and he applied artificial respiration for an hour before the man came around.

For their heroism, Congress awarded gold life-saving medals to Keeper Longstreet, John Andersen, and Charles Bowker, plus a silver medal to Harry Andersen.

"The Worst Days of a Bad Fall": Captain Motley and the Surfmen of Middle Island In November 1911

by Eric C. Hartlep
(Volume 7, Issue 3)

By the time the gales of November 1911 arrived, the lifesavers of Middle Island (Michigan) had already logged more than their share of trouble. Even before the active season began, Captain Eugene P. Motley found himself short-handed.

"Surfman W. J. McCafferey telephoned that he would not be back," Motley wrote on March 11th, "as he had a position in a lighthouse." Ten days later, Surfman Frank A. Paschke also resigned. With Station 253 set to open on April 12th, the sudden death of Surfman Peter Poirer's father meant the No. 2 surfman would be detained on the mainland. This left a crew consisting only of Keeper Motley and five permanent surfmen: Jake Hauck, Louis Candy, George Cottenham, George Hartlep, and Ernest Saint Onge.

Between May and October, the depleted crew - filled out with temporary men and the 16-year-old legal ward of Captain Motley, Fred Scarborough - handled the grounding of the 2,005-ton steamer *City of London*, and the disabled 4,795-ton steamer *James S. Durham*. They also rescued those aboard the yachts *Janet* and *Jahana* - the *Janet's* during what Motley called "The worst storm of the season" on July 24th.

But the worst summer storm would be nothing compared to November's fury. Eugene Motley's log for the first of the month painted a frigid picture: "Practiced with signals and service code. Snowed all day, quite cold. Regular winter weather." Only twenty steamers passed by Middle Island. The following day, Motley decided against having his men practice with the beach apparatus, "as ground was covered with snow and frequent snow squalls. Ice formed along the shore a little last night." Two days later, he reported: "The spark plugs on motor in life boat are all short circuited and could not get spark sufficient to operate engine."

By November 5th, with spark plugs bought in town at a 50% discount, the lifeboat was operational again, and would soon be needed. Fifty steamers passed the island that day, though all of them survived the increasing winds. It was the 30-year-old schooner *John Mee* - a wooden, 199-ton vessel of a type almost extinct on the Great Lakes - that demanded Middle Island's attention. On the morning of November 7th, Captain Motley "received telephone message from Presque Isle light that a schooner with flag half-masted was coming down the lake. At 8:40 AM the schooner came in sight. Called crew, launched lifeboat, which on account of low water (in harbor), caused a little delay… had to move around inside of island to head her off on south side of island."

The aging vessel, with a five-man crew and no cargo, was on its way from Tobermory, Canada, to Raber, Michigan. Motley stated that "While off 40-Mile Point, 7 miles north of Roger City, (the schooner) was struck by NW gale and big seas, which caused mizzen mast to break off about 5 feet from the deck, and in its fall struck the boat davits on starboard side, breaking rail of yawl, and then going overboard. They had to cut it loose in order to save the vessel, thereby loosing all sails and rigging on the mizzen. Also broke off top of main topmast above the stays, and tearing the mainsail badly."

With so much damage, the ship was lucky to be afloat. Motley secured a towline and ran the vessel down the lake, to an anchorage on the leeward side of Middle Island. "Then went to Turnbull's Mill and requested a tug by telephone to come from Alpena and tow them to harbor. Tug arrived 3:45 PM, helped to get up anchor and they left for Alpena, and I returned to station at 5 PM. The schooner's hull was not damaged, but the loss will be about $1000. The lifeboat engine worked well until high tension wire on forward cylinder burnt and broke off. And not having any spare we had to return to station on 3 cylinders. It was a rough day, big sea and gale of wind. The captain was well please[d] with assistance rendered by this crew, and glad when I told him I had secured a tug for him, as his vessel was unable come in, stay, or work to windward with the little canvas left, (only) stay sail plus reefed foresail and a piece of mainsail."

The gale that wrecked *John Mee* continued unabated, threatening even more vessels over the coming week, according to several *Alpena Argus-Pioneer* stories. "A terrific storm swept over the lakes Saturday night and Sunday, a climax to a week's stormy and disagreeable weather... The wind blew 42 miles an hour here and 48 miles at Middle Island. Temperatures started to go down after the thunderstorm about 9 o'clock Saturday evening. Many cellars were flooded with water." Under the headline "Lighter Ashore" the paper reported that "A lighter owned by Captain Gillingham went on the beach at Middle Island Sunday. The lighter was brought to the island Saturday, towed by a gasoline launch. The launch could not get the lighter away on account of the storm and Captain Gillingham was obliged to return to Presque Isle harbor. Captain Motley found it necessary to scuttle the lighter in order to prevent the lighter from beating the lifeboat dock to pieces." The *Argus* failed to mention that the lighter had grounded, then gone sideways on a reef, or that, by Motley's account, the gasoline tug - not a launch - "was being rapidly drawn on the reef so had to cut tow line as tug was striking bottom."

After months of work put in by his crew building the lifeboat dock, Motley surely was not about to stand by and watch it destroyed. Especially by what was essentially a barge, valued at only $200, with no crew aboard, and a cargo of 175 fish net stakes. Captain Gillingham was no stranger to disaster when approaching Middle Island, having run aground with his gasoline scow *Molly Hogan* while attempting to deliver cord wood to the station on July 27th of the previous year. In that incident, the Middle Island crew worked almost until midnight to free the wreck, stopping only when "some of the men were nearly perished by the cold water," according to Motley. This time, being later in the year, conditions were even colder. "The tug had a crew of 3 and they were thankful for assistance rendered as had to work in the water with ice forming all the time. Neither lifeboat nor surfboat used. A small boat, 16ft skiff, made 6 trips on the three days. Vessel saved; damage $50. All cargo saved."

Between mishaps, Captain Motley did his best to get days off for his crew during the continuing storms that November. It was a chancy proposition, as there was no guarantee a man on leave could return if a ship was in distress. On November 17th, harsh weather trapped temporary Surfman James Starr on the mainland. That left only six of the crew - surfmen Collins, St. Onge, Poirier, Hauck, Cottenham and Hartlep - to man the boats. Motley had no choice but to employ 16 year-old Fred Scarborough as lookout. The move paid off when Scarborough spotted the steamer *Isabel J. Boyce* at 1 p.m., as she "came under the island and hoisted distress flag."

Ever since sunrise, surf around Middle Island had been very high, with alternating rain and snow as temperatures hovered around freezing. "The steamer *Isabel J. Boyce*," reads the station log, "while coming up lake before a SE gale, with barge *William A. Young* in tow ... (when) south of island, tow line to barge parted and barge went adrift. The sea was so big that in trying to turn about, decks filled with water and steamer was in danger of foundering. They cut holes in bulwarks to let water out, threw over 50 tons of soft coal they had on deck and ran under island and called us out." Besides a hold filling with water, the crew of the steamer faced a ruptured boiler, which they patched together with a "rolling brace." There was also a steam pipe leak. They found shelter below Middle Island, expecting repairs to take "a few hours." With *Boyce* safely anchored, her captain, Robert C. Pringle, was more concerned with the fate of Captain Alex McLean and the six-man crew aboard *William A. Young*, a 28-year-old partly-dismasted schooner now used as a barge. But until reaching *Boyce*, and talking to Pringle, Captain Motley had been unaware another ship was involved. Because of extremely high waves, the only chance of reaching the foundering barge in the station's lifeboat was to be towed there by the steamer.

Once alongside, however, Motley found the old schooner deserted, "the crew having left in yawl boat." Still, Captain Pringle "wished us to try and board barge and get anchor down. Started to go aboard, but could not get on, the steamer not stopping to help or stand by, but she started for shelter as soon as they let go of us." The men of Station 253 were left on their own, far from home in a fierce storm. "As I could do nothing in big sea," wrote Motley, "returned to station, having to pull about 3 miles against sea and wind, which took us nearly two hours, arriving at station 6 PM. Big sea, terrible day."

"The barge continued to drift before gale," the keeper wrote later, in his wreck report book. "At 8 PM heard over telephone that crew of barge in yawl boat had landed at Nine Mile Point, 4 1/2 miles south of station after a very rough trip and had left for Alpena." Once in town, the crew's story of their ordeal made front-page news in the *Argus-Pioneer*: "After the tow line parted, the crew of the *Young* battled as best they could. The foremast was down, had snapped off, leaving about a third standing. The mast and rigging, a useless mass of wreckage, were fouled under the bow. Heavy seas were washing over the barge. Captain McLean and crew undertook to pull in the parted towline and fasten it to the wreckage astern, in order to steady the barge. However, this could not be accomplished.

"The *Young* was slowly settling. Her seams were parting. In one place three 12-inch planks were torn from her side. The yawl boat might be washed overboard at any moment, so the crew decided it would be safer to abandon the barge and take to the yawl boat, although this was taking an awful chance."

After a few days to reflect on events, Captain Motley completed his final report. It seems doubtful, from the tone of his account, that Motley agreed with the *Argus-Pioneer* that the steamer's captain had done all it could that day, or indeed the next, to save its barge. "The captain of *Boyce* wanted us to go with him in morning [of November 18th] and look for barge. The gale continued shifting to NW with snow squalls. The steamer did not wait for us, but pulled up under False Presque Isle Point 6 miles NW for shelter and did not call for us."

The next day, November 19th, the steamer left for Alpena. Her captain phoned Middle Island around 10 a.m., to inform Motley he "would not leave to look for the boat until Monday morning, 20th, when [he] would call the crew at Thunder Bay Island, the barge having drifted down the lake before the NW gale." *William A. Young* would now be the worry of Captain Persons, a dozen miles to the south at Station 252. While Captain Motley certainly wished the Thunder Bay Island men no trouble, he must have been glad to wash his hands of the entire affair.

Person's crew was to be spared a repeat of Middle Island's trials, though at the cost of a sunken vessel. From Motley's log: "November 21st (Captain Persons) reported that the steamer *Boyce* and Thunder

Bay Island crew found some wreckage yesterday, that would indicated that barge had sank." *William A. Young* was a total loss.

Still, there was yet more trouble brewing for the Middle Island crew. On November 24th, "Surfman Candy received word that his father was not expected to live and left 2:30 PM for town." Candy would not return. With the season of Great Lakes navigation nearing its end, and his father deathly ill, he decided to end his career on Middle Island. Down again to only six men, Captain Motley re-activated young Fred Scarborough as a substitute. In only three days time, the boy would find himself alone at the station - except for Elizabeth Motley, the keeper's blind and crippled sister - for nearly two full days, while the lifesavers fought to save a stranded tug. "The steamer *Fairmount*," reported the *Argus-Pioneer*, "bound from Harbor Beach to Muskegon, with a big scow in tow, went aground on a reef near Presque Isle light about 3 o'-clock Monday afternoon [November 27th]. The Middle Island life savers went to the relief of the tug about 7 o'clock and remained with the crew during the night."

Yet it was not as easy a voyage to *Fairmount*, and the lighter she was towing, as the papers made it sound. Three miles from the station, according to Motley's account, the surfboat "broke eccentric rod to water pump and engine would not run. Put on sail and oars and continued as had fair wind, arriving at tug at 10:40 PM. Tried to tow lighter but could not, worked until 1 AM."

This rescue would be all manpower, not gasoline horsepower, and the site of the wreck was 16 miles distant from Middle Island. Around 5 a.m. on the 28th, the wind shifted somewhat, and using sail and oar the surfmen succeeded in pulling the lighter to safety, anchoring her nearby. That part settled, the crew ran a line to the tug, and using a winch on the anchored lighter and the tug's working engine, were able to pull *Fairmount* free as well at 10:15 a.m. However, with the weather "blowing a gale from NE, rain turning to snow and as could not return to station with disabled boat in gale," Motley reported, he and his crew laid up "until 7 AM November 29th, when hauled boat alongside tug and by using hot water got ice off boat and outfit, so could handle boat and left 8 AM for station."

Even with their work done, getting home again would not be an easy venture for the Middle Island crew. "The wind having hauled to west," wrote Motley, "wind kept freshening and hauling to SW so that did not arrive at station until 12:15 PM. Having been 4 hours making 16 miles. It was one the most severe gales of the season, rain turning to snow and freezing hard. Lifeboat was covered with ice and everything frozen. The damage to the tug would not exceed $500 while damage to the lifeboat consisted of one starboard light washed overboard and lost one oarlock and two oarlocks busted."

The *Argus-Pioneer* summed up the rescue and the season in an article in their December 6th issue, stating that "It was one of the worst days of a bad fall. The life savers had a rough trip going over in the life boat and the return was no pleasure trip. They were absent from the island about 40 hours, the longest they have been absent since the season opened." At least the master of *Fairmount*, Captain Louis Larsen, had done all he could to aid the surfmen helping him, even going so far as to furnish them hot meals over the three days.

Considering the sheer number of rescues that November and the severity of the weather, the Middle Island crew probably gave no thought to the possibility that the *Fairmount's* rescue would be their last that year, yet it was. Through the first week of December winds were light, and even with an average of fifty steamers a day passing their lookouts, not one would need their help.

As it became more certain the active season was drawing to a close, the men began to take steps in preparation for a winter away from the island. First, the crewmen's trunks were taken to town, then the station's cooks - Annie Olson and another local woman - were sent to the mainland. On December 4th, the station's inner harbor froze, forming the first banks around the island. Just three steamers passed by on the 14th, and two days later Motley received the expected telegram: "Harbor Beach Dec 16. Keeper Middle Island Station. Close station this day, Dec 16. Signed, Kiah." The men left at midnight for the mainland and home, glad for the end of their worst fall ever.

Columbia River Gold Rush: The Rescue of the Rosecrans

by Frederick Stonehouse
(Volume 8, Issue 2)

Comparatively few life-saving stations were built on the Pacific coast; five in Washington, six in Oregon, eight in California and one in Alaska. Perhaps the single one in Alaska was there just so she didn't feel left out!

It wasn't that shipwrecks were any less prevalent or deadly on the west coast, but rather as the Life-Saving Service developed it moved from east to west, growing and expanding as it went. By the time it reached the Pacific the nature of shipping and the resulting shipwrecks were changing. Less and less frequently did they go up on outer bars within range of shore-based lifeboat crews. More commonly they sank farther offshore, beyond the life-savers range.

By any standard the life-savers' effort to rescue the crew of the steamer *Rosecrans* is among the most spectacular in service history. It is one of only two instances where crews from two stations received gold medals for the same rescue. The only other example is the wreck of the L.C. Waldo on Lake Superior in 1913.

The *Rosecrans* was a 29 year-old, 2,976-ton bulk oil freighter owned by the Associated Oil Company. She was bound from Monterey, California, to Portland, Oregon, with 19,000 barrels of crude oil when she ran up on Peacock Spit at the entrance to the Columbia River, Oregon, just after 5:00 a.m. on January 7, 1913. The steamer and cargo were valued at $260,000.

Unfortunately, a very heavy gale was screaming, which would ultimately kill not only the steamer but also 30 of the 33-man crew. It was one of the worst disasters on the infamous Columbia Bar.

RESCUE

The *Rosecrans* departed Monterey the afternoon of January 4 and had an easy run up the coast until the night of the 6th when she approached the Columbia River. Captain L. F. Johnson planned to linger off the bar until the morning and cross at first light when tidal conditions would be better. The Columbia River bar was notoriously rough and difficult to cross. Waiting until daylight was a good decision.

Navigation on the *Rosecrans* was evidently a bit "off." One of the two survivors, Quartermaster John Slinning, stated she passed Tillamook Rock Light "a little before 4:00 a.m. on the 7th," and that she was running at slow speed a mile and half or two and a half miles off shore, steering eight degrees. The weather was terrible, with a 60-70 miles per hour southerly gale accompanied with heavy following sea. Rain and mist obscured vision. A second quartermaster, William Peters, who also survived, testified when he relieved Slinning about 4:00 a.m., he saw a white light off the starboard bow, believed to be Cape Disappointment. A second light visible a half-point on the starboard bow was thought to be North Head. The Columbia River Lightship was not sighted. The captain made a short appearance on deck just after 4:00 a.m. and exchanged a few words with the Third Officer, C. R. Palmer, but the steamer kept to her course. Captain Johnson was considered a good and capable man as well as a skilled navigator.

Unraveling how the modern, well-found tanker ended up on a well-known hazard was difficult to determine, especially since most of the principals were dead. However the investigating officer determined, "No other conclusion can be reached by me than that the disaster resulted from poor judgment and carelessness on the part of those who were responsible for the navigation and safety of the *Rosecrans*. The vessel must have passed Tillamook Rock Light earlier than 3:30 a.m. as it is unreasonable to think that she could have covered 19 nautical miles in the next hour and 40 minutes under slow bell. If the course steered is correct, unless the compass was greatly in error, the light abeam must have been much more than 2 1/2 miles distant, otherwise the vessel would have stranded on Clatsop Beach."

Captain Johnson should have remained on deck approaching the Columbia River bar at night under such unfavorable weather conditions and stood a course sufficiently broad to make the lightship and carry his vessel outside of danger."[1]

Peacock Spit, the bar he stranded on, takes its name from the U.S. Sloop of War Peacock which stranded on it in 1841. The spit is located southwest of Baker Bay and south of North Head. Many other ships also met their end on the spit. Once a ship goes up, she is either pounded to death by the waves or swallowed whole by the soft quicksand. The end is the same. The surf on the spit is always heavy, but rarely as bad as it was the morning the *Rosecrans* went up. The actual point the steamer struck is roughly a mile and a half from shore and about the same distance southwest of the Cape Disappointment Life-Saving Station.

As soon as the *Rosecrans* shuddered to a stop the captain ordered the radio operator to send out an S.O.S., stating she was on the bar and breaking up. The operator repeated the message three or four times before the captain told him not to broadcast any more. He was afraid the sparks would ignite the cargo. Before being ordered to stop, L. T. Crow, the wireless operator at Astoria replied, "O.K, Will send help. About where are you?" The *Rosecrans* sent back, "Water has entered the cabins - I can't stay much longer - hel-..." The critical question, "where are you?" wasn't answered. It would be the cause of many needless deaths.

Keeper Oscar Wicklund of the Point Adams Life-Saving Station believed if the location were immediately known the life-savers could have rescued the majority of the *Rosecrans* sailors. Wicklund was a veteran life-saver, appointed keeper in 1898 and still serving when the Coast Guard was born in 1915. The life-saving boats could have passed through the cutoff and out past Cape Disappointment and McKenzie Head safely since it was slack water. Also, a man wearing a lifejacket would have drifted towards shore where the life-savers' boats could have more easily fished him out of the water. If only a location was given in the first radio S.O.S., much loss of life could have been avoided. Keeper Rimer from the Cape Disappointment Station agreed with Wicklund's reasoning.

S. S. Gilbert, the government wireless operator at North Head, also received the transmissions. As soon as the Astoria station ceased broadcasting he repeated the distress message. He also tried to telephone the Cape Disappointment Life-Saving Station, but the telephone lines were down.

Captain Johnson immediately ordered reverse engines and the tanker began to slide off the spit. He also ordered the pumps started to jettison cargo in an effort to lighten the ship. Progress was short lived. A series of monster seas slammed into her, tearing off her hatches, flooding below decks and drowning her boiler fires. The water shorted out her lights, plunging the freighter into darkness.

Other than the brief radio traffic, no effort was made to call for help. The survivors were unaware if she even carried any flares or rockets. The whistle was never blown since the engine room flooded almost immediately, thus robbing it of the necessary steam. Lifejackets were on board but not all of the crew bothered to wear them. Her four lifeboats were carried away by the waves nearly as soon as she struck. They would have been useless anyway, given the ferocity of the waves.

The crew assembled amidships below decks, an area sheltered from the grasping waves, and waited for rescue. They knew the ship radioed an S.O.S. and all assumed help would soon be on the way. The thundering Columbia waves continued to pound the helpless ship. Just before dawn the foremast carried away and soon the *Rosecrans* broke in two just abaft it. The crew stayed under shelter until almost 9 a.m. when they were finally driven to the open decks.

Since there were only three survivors from the wreck, knowledge of what actually happened aboard her is limited at best. At the official investigation, survivor Fred Peters, aged 30 years, testified to the confusion on the wreck and how he lived to tell the tale, "When I was on deck I tried to make the wheelhouse, where most of the crew were and when I got forward of the stack I met Captain Johnson. He was trying to get up to the wheelhouse too but his leg was broken, so we got him on the fiddley under the overhang of the house. The seas were coming so strong that the after end of the house began to sag, so we had to get out of there. When I got out a sea washed me to the rail. When the sea cleared I tried to make the rigging but missed it and fell on the main deck. The next sea took me overboard. I noticed a plank a few feet away and swam to it. I drifted over toward North Head Light and I thought I was safe until I saw the rocks and the breakers. I tried to swim clear of the rocks and it seems the current started to take me out to sea. I then drifted up to the north'ard and the breakers got me and took me ashore. I lost my plank when I got into the breakers. I was obligated to cut my life preserver, as it got over my head. I stayed on top of the breakers as best I could all the way in and then crawled up on the driftwood away from the sea."[2]

It took five and a half hours to drift ashore but he won his impossible wager with death. One of the soldiers from nearby Fort Stevens found him and carried him to a local house with the help of others. There he was given restoratives. Keeper Theodore Conick of the Klipsan Beach Life-Saving Station rushed to his aid in an automobile, stripped him, rubbed him down for about an hour and a half, gave him hot stimulants and put him to bed.

When the ship hit the spit, Quartermaster Slinning, another survivor, ran to the bridge. "There were a number of men besides myself on the bridge. As the big seas lifted the bridge and pilothouse off, I first grabbed the exhaust pipe, held on to that for a while, then got around the after part of the smokestack. A sea struck me from there and sent me over the rail. I held onto the rail until the sea passed. Then another sea took me to the after rail and I got up into the main rigging."[3]

The quartermaster said he saw "quite a number" washed over. Besides Slinning, two other men, Carpenter Erick Lundmark and S. Cagna from the engine room managed to climb into the rigging. Slinning and Lundmark would eventually be rescued by the Point Adams Life-Saving Station crew and therein is an epic tale of courage, heroism and just plain "guts."

It is assumed the 30 crewmen who didn't survive perished when the bridge and wheelhouse were swept into the sea.

When the operator at Astoria received the *Rosecrans'* S.O.S. he immediately sent out a general distress call. He failed to get a response from any station, but instead of doing nothing, he called Mr. V. Boelling, the Puget Sound Tugboat Company agent at Astoria, and requested him to tell the life-saving stations at Cape Disappointment and Point Adams. The tug agent also got the message to Point Adams Station.

Putting this all in perspective, it wasn't until 8:40 a.m., over three and a half hours after the *Rosecrans* went up on Peacock Spit, that anyone on shore knew where the wreck actually was! It was then Surfman Fry, the lookout at Cape Disappointment, on the ocean side of the cape and a quarter mile from the station, sighted a steamer supposedly anchored in the breakers off McKenzie Head. The weather was thick and rainy and he could not see more than half a mile but at

The Point Adams Life-Saving Station crew poses with the motor lifeboat Dreadnaught *on October 23, 1916. United States Coast Guard photo.*

8:40 a.m. he spotted the smokestack and mast of a ship apparently anchored. The lookout quickly called Keeper Alfred Rimer who hurried to the tower to see for himself. He didn't see much. The steamer was obscured by the mist and barely visible. He saw no distress signals and her bow appeared to be down. Nonetheless, she must be the elusive *Rosecrans*, so he called back to the station and ordered the motor lifeboat *Tenacious* readied. They would leave as soon as he returned.

The crew first tried to go directly around the cape but the gale was too strong and, combined with the flooding tide, was more than the lifeboat could handle. As an alternative, they ran out using the cut between Sand Island and the eastern end of Peacock Spit, but the surf was still too severe and after an hour of trying they were unable to reach the steamer. Rimer hailed a passing tug, the *Tatoosh*, asking for a tow over the bar but Captain Reed refused, unwilling to risk it, saying, "it was a crazy idea to try to cross the bar." Refusing to give up, Rimer tried again and this time was able with great difficulty to battle out over the Republic Spit but could go no further. Reluctantly he swung around and returned to wait for slack water, reaching the station at about 11:30 a.m.

Not long after Rimer and his crew returned, they were surprised to see Keeper Oscar S. Wicklund and his Point Adams crew arrive in their motor lifeboat *Dreadnaught*. The tug agent at Astoria managed to get a message through to Wicklund at 5:30 a.m. about the wreck. He also told him the tug *Tatoosh* was going to try to reach the wreck. The agent erroneously told the Keeper the *Rosecrans* was likely in the breakers at Clatsop Spit, a long sand bank running northwest from the south side of the river mouth. Wicklund took action. He sent surfman Allan to patrol the beach to see if the wreck was indeed on Clatsop Spit and telephoned the jetty foreman at Point Adams asking him to run an engine out to see what he could. The jetty reached seaward and was a good coastal vantage point. He also ordered the *Dreadnaught* out for a search.

Wicklund and his crew first went to the river mouth where they met Captain Reed and the *Tatoosh*. The faster tug checked the Clatsop Spit but found nothing. They returned to the station where they learned the reports from the patrol and jetty were both negative.

The life-savers were men of action. It was not their habit to sit and wait for things to come to them. They took action instead.

Wicklund decided to run across the Columbia River to check with the Cape Disappointment crew, thus their unexpected arrival. Since telephone service was out, the lifeboat trip was the only way to coordinate actions. Just as the *Dreadnaught* was about to pull away from her slip, he received a telephone message from Fort Stevens telling him she was aground on Peacock Spit. Evidently the information came from the quartermaster found ashore by the soldier. Realizing the criticality of coordinating their actions, Wicklund ran over to the Cape Disappointment Station to find Keeper Rimer.

Perhaps to further reconnoiter the wreck, Wicklund and *Dreadnaught* set out for the wreck while *Tenacious* remained at the station. Wicklund later wrote, "All that could be seen of the wreck was the mast sticking up with three men clinging to the rigging. I did not have much hope of reaching the vessel but thought it would encourage those men in the rigging if they saw the lifeboat constantly trying to reach them. I made two attempts, but the boat was entirely submerged and we were forced to return. I got out only a quarter of a mile from the cape.

"When I got back to the Cape Disappointment Station, I talked the matter over with Capt. Rimer, and we agreed that we must reach the vessel if there was any way for us to do so. We concluded we must make another attempt right away, the tide having slackened. We made up our minds that we would not quit trying as long as there was anyone left in the rigging."[4]

Wicklund's narrative continued: "We left the station together about 12:30 p.m. [author's note - Rimer says 1:00 p.m.] Capt. Rimer's boat was about 200 yards ahead of mine, due to the fact that he was running at full speed. I slowed down a little against every sea to save my boat from destruction. While the wind had hauled a little to the southwest and moderated somewhat, it was still blowing a gale. The seas filled our boat constantly."

Spectators on shore report the breakers were stupendous and washed over the pair constantly. Regardless, the two lifeboats kept going.

"I observed the Cape Disappointment boat [*Tenacious*] go out between the wreck and the shore, circle around the bow of the ship and then run to a position to southward of her. They seemed to be in trouble as they lay in the same position a while.

"The wreck was lying heading west. I ran in as close as I dared toward the starboard quarter and signaled to the men in the rigging to jump, that being in my opinion the only way in which they could be rescued. I circled five times and got as near the vessel as I dared each time, signaling to the sailors to jump, but they would not do it. As we got near the wreck the fifth time, a terrific sea struck our boat, turning it almost end over end and washing five members of the crew overboard, including myself. We all managed to hang on to the life rails and were hauled back into the boat - all except Surfman Pearson. When the boat righted itself he was more than 300 yards away from us. We had no difficulty however in picking him up. At this point we observed the Cape Disappointment crew signaling for assistance. We responded and found they also had suffered a capsize, which had damaged their boat and stopped their engine. We towed them to the tug *Fearless*, which was standing by outside the breakers. We then returned to the wreck. Just as soon as we got within about 100 yards of the vessel, one of the men jumped and was quickly rescued. This was Erick Lundmark, the ship's carpenter. Then another man - John Slinning - jumped and was rescued in the same manner. There was still another man in the rigging but he was hanging from the ratlines and appeared to be dead. He fell shortly afterwards, struck an iron stanchion and dropped into the sea. We picked up the body as it drifted toward us.

"It was now about 4 o'clock. The sea was still high and the tide running out strong. We had no chance to return to the harbor. We set our course for the Columbia River Lightship, several miles seaward. We arrived there at 7:30 p.m.

"On account of the heavy sea, we experienced considerable difficulty in getting aboard the lightship. We let the boat astern on 50 fathoms of 4-inch rope. The following morning the wind had increased instead of moderated and the sea was mountain high. The life-saving crew, with the aid of the officers and men of the lightship, tried three different times during the day to haul the boat alongside to get the remains of the sailor and free the boat of water, but the gale and sea made it impossible to do so without running the risk of killing someone. At 9:00 p.m. it was found the boat had gone adrift."[5]

Some of the lifeboat crew thought the hawser may have fouled the submarine bell and chafed until it finally broke. The boat was in terrible shape. The after bulkhead was leaking and the men constantly used the bilge pump in a futile effort to clear her of water. What really happened to the waterlogged and broken boat will never be known.

By contrast with Rimer's balky engine, Wicklund's ran well, continuing to operate even when the boat capsized. The motor lifeboats were designed to run even if they rolled but the difference between theory and fact in the midst of a Columbia Bar shipwreck can be a wide gap. Wicklund's engineman was young Leonard Pearson, temporary surfman number 8. It was a vital job for such a junior man but evidently the keeper knew Pearson's capability well.

The local tugboats played an important part in the rescue effort. The *Oneonta*, with Captain Charles E. Anderson, went over the bar in the morning in an unsuccessful attempt to find the *Rosecrans*. She went out again later in the afternoon to look for the Point Adams crew, reported missing and disabled. When night fell she fired rockets and burned blue lights as signals without success. About midnight she found them on the lightship but the seas were too severe to take them off. They hung around the lightship all night, but the next day the seas were still too stormy so she returned to Astoria. A third try on the 9th proved the charm and she brought them in to Astoria where a large crowd greeted rescued and rescuers alike.

Captain E. D. Parsons and the tug *Fearless* lived up to her name, searching for the steamer on the morning of the wreck without success. She again went out in the afternoon and luckily was on the scene when the Cape Disappointment boat was disabled, taking her in tow from the *Dreadnaught*. Wicklund advised the *Fearless* to leave the area quickly, expressing concern he didn't want to have to deal with two shipwrecks.

For a while the *Fearless* kept position about 400 yards westward of the *Rosecrans*. Her captain claimed the waves were so high at times they completely hid the men in the rigging from view. He thought it impossible for a lifeboat to reach the wreck and make the rescue.

Rimer and *Tenacious* were having major problems. On the way out the boat sprang a bad leak and the engine broke twice. It could be kept running, but the speed could not be throttled back to slow. Regardless of his trouble, the keeper ran the boat within 20 feet of the wreck and encouraged the men in the rigging to jump. Having no success, Rimer lay the boat off about 50 yards from the *Rosecrans* to wait out a series of enormous seas. At precisely the wrong moment, his balky engine quit! With a dead engine they were defenseless and capsized by one of the waves. Rimer and two of his crew were washed out and the boat's steering gear and rudder disabled. When the boat went over, Rimer held on to the steel lifeline so tightly the brass stanchion broke in two and his hand was badly cut from the wire. Surfman de Kruis had his leg bruised badly enough to later require hospitalization. All were able to regain the boat. The keeper later wrote; "After a few minutes we all managed by the greatest effort to get on board again but found the boat and engine room full of water. We never-the-less manned the oars and tried our best to get back to the wreck. But not withstanding our utmost efforts, we failed. As we were in a seething cauldron and unable to handle our boat with oars, I wigwagged to the Point Adams boat to tow us into quieter water and Capt. Wicklund came and towed us to the tug *Fearless*. We tried to pump our boat out, but it was no use. Her bottom was all split up and her air compartments full of water."[6]

The difficulty faced by the lifeboats can be gleaned from comments made by Keeper Rimer in his official report. "The seas were confused, going in every direction. One time Capt. Wicklund's boat was headed into a sea which appeared to be 40 feet high. It struck the *Dreadnaught*

This photo, from the Coast Guard Historian's Office, is clearly labeled "Point Adams" in the top lefthand corner, yet yields no further identification as to the names of the members of the crew. United States Coast Guard photo.

broadside and I thought he was gone. I started to go to his assistance, but when I looked again I found he was all right."[7]

The *Fearless* began to tow the boat into harbor but had gone only a short distance when Captain Parsons became concerned the *Tenacious* wouldn't survive the rough trip over the bar as the boat appeared to have little or no buoyancy. It didn't help that the bottom was split, her air tanks full of water and water an inch above her decks. Since the life-savers were dog tired and still in the boat his concern was understandable. Surfman Allen of Point Adams was aboard the *Fearless*, having been left ashore when the lifeboat departed, offered to go aboard the *Tenacious* to help steer her during the crossing but Parsons refused to let him. Instead he brought all the boat crew to the tug. This proved a very wise decision. Going over the bar the towline broke and the drifting boat rolled over and over. Rimer estimated she capsized five or six times. In the prevailing gale conditions, Parsons made no attempt to pick her up. Conditions were too extreme to risk lives for a mere boat.

The pure courage displayed by the life-savers was incredible. On the way back in with the Cape Disappointment crew, Captain Parsons overheard a remarkable conversation, the gist of which follows: "Keeper Rimer told his men that if they could not get a gasoline launch they would take the Dobbins lifeboat at Pt. Adams and pull over to Ft. Canby that night. Some of the crew said they thought this would be a very dangerous undertaking on account of the weather and tidal conditions. They would obey the order and follow him to the end, even if it cost them their lives. Keeper Rimer said, 'Boys that's what we are paid for.'"[8]

Captain Parsons had his own measure of courage. Minutes after hearing the life-savers exchange he received a telegram from the tug company telling him the Point Adams lifeboat was disabled and had three survivors aboard. He wirelessed back, "It is dark and the bar is breaking heavy but I will return." After assuring all his deck gear was again fully secured he headed for the bar. His towing pennant double lashed, doors and skylights secured, ventilators turned from the seas and all men accounted for. His first trip over the bar took an hour with combers breaking over the tug constantly. There was no reason to think this crossing would be any different. He had a large group of people aboard, not only his own crew but also the Cape Disappointment crew, totaling 24 men. Before he reached the bar another telegram informed him the tug *Oneonta* was going out. He could come home. When the *Oneonta* came up, Parsons passed her his supply of Coston signals. Parsons dropped the life-savers off at the Point Adams Station as they asked for.

Neither the Cape Disappointment or Point Adams lifeboats were ever recovered.

One of the sidelight questions the wreck helped answer concerned the value of "putting oil on troubled waters." Did oil really help calm the seas? Since the *Rosecrans* carried a cargo of oil and the ship had broken open, a fair amount was released. Did it do any good? The question was put to Keeper Wicklund during the investigation. There was a streak of oil about 20 feet wide running from wreck toward the shore. "Question - 'Did the oil seem to smooth the seas?' Answer - 'Yes indeed. Had it not been for the oil I do not think the men in the rigging would have jumped, because they followed that streak when they came towards the boat.'"[9]

Few of the crew's bodies were ever recovered although the life-savers made extensive beach patrols. Strong currents carried them out to sea.

The spectacular rescue drew wide attention to the life-savers. Representative L.O. Belland of the Oregon Legislature introduced, and the Legislature passed, a resolution of appreciation and thanks to both crews. What made it especially noteworthy was Belland spent 18 months as a surfman, so well understood the Life-Saving Service and its motto, "Regulations say we have to go out. They say nothing about coming back."

The Point Adams crew was a wreck-tested group. Four of the men participated in rescuing the entire crew of the steamer Ireland in 1907. The crew also proved very innovative as exemplified by the wreck of the four-masted schooner Admiral on January 13, 1912. It started when Wicklund received a radio call from a tanker that a schooner was in trouble off the south jetty. The Columbia River has long rock jetties on both the north and south entrances. Since the bar was impassable, ruling out the use of the lifeboat, he arranged to travel to the jetty and out on it via the steam locomotive used to repair it. In the 70-mph gale and thrashing seas there was danger the trestle would be swept away, but he and the engine crew continued on until they found the schooner captain crawling along on his hands and knees carrying his nearly frozen-to-death infant. The fog was so thick they nearly missed seeing him even though he was next to the rails. The captain implored them to continue

The Point Adams Life-Saving Station crew performs their weekly lifeboat drill for a gathered crowd. The motor lifeboat Dreadnaught *(not pictured here) was lost during the* Rosecrans *rescue. United States Coast Guard photo.*

on and find his wife somewhere behind him. They did and she was still alive. Just down the tracks from her they found the cook and bundled him aboard the train. Realizing he needed more help, as well as his equipment, Wicklund and the train returned three miles to Fort Stevens and loaded his crew complete with Lyle gun and related gear. When all was ready they headed back down the trestle looking for the schooner. Just past the three-mile mark, still running in thick fog, they stopped just short of a 200-foot gap the waves smashed through the wood structure. Had the train engineer not been extra vigilant, they could have driven off into the gap. On the opposite side was the rest of the schooner crew but no ship. Quickly the life-savers fired a line across the chasm and the breeches buoy was soon in operation, bringing the half frozen men to safety. The schooner was later found on a bar out by Peacock Spit. She proved a total loss.

Fort Stevens, mentioned several times previously, was one of a string of Army forts designed to protect the Columbia River area from attack. Fort Stevens was established in 1863 with new batteries added as situations dictated. It has the distinction of being the only seacoast fort in the contiguous states attacked by a foreign power since the War of 1812, when it was shelled by a Japanese submarine in 1942.

The *Rosecrans* was known as a "hard luck" ship, always seeming to suffer breakdowns, strandings and other mishaps. On March 12, 1912 she was thrown on the rocks off Alcatraz Island in California's San Francisco Bay resulting in a 25-foot hole in her hull. Two sailors died trying to launch a lifeboat. Once considered unsalvageable, she was recovered and back in service in six months. On August 27, 1912 she suffered an explosion and fire at Gaviolta, California. It cost nearly as much to rebuild her as original construction. She was built in Glasgow, Scotland in 1884.

While the loss of the *Rosecrans* is one of the worst shipwrecks in Life-Saving Service history, the crews' efforts during the disaster are also among the most exemplary. The iron endurance of the life-savers was incredible. Seldom have life-saving crews fought against worse odds or showed a more indomitable spirit. In recognition of their efforts, the Secretary of the Treasury awarded Gold Live-Saving Medals to the members of each crew.

SECTION IV:
Enter The Coast Guard

THE FIRST RESCUE: THE WRECK OF THE SYLVIA C. HALL

by CDR. John F. Ebersole, USCG (Ret.)
(Volume 6, Issue 3)

Chief Warrant Officer Freddie G. Gilliken, born in 1878, was the oldest living Coast Guard officer at the time of the interview upon which this article is based (April 1975). The son of the owner of a small fleet of coastal schooners, Fred Gilliken at twenty-one turned down his father's offer to name him master of the fleet's newest schooner. The challenge of lifesaving work proved to be a stronger calling. Three years later, in 1904, Gilliken joined the United States Life-Saving Service. In 1915 the Life-Saving Service merged with the U.S. Revenue Cutter Service to form the present United States Coast Guard. This story recounts one of the first rescues to occur after this merger.

At 0400 Wednesday, 17 March 1915, the English cook employed by the crew of Cape Lookout (NC) Coast Guard Station arose. A shipwreck survivor with a special debt to the former U.S. Life-Saving Service, he set about preparing breakfast. He noted that the weather had taken a turn for the worse during the night. A howling southeast gale was competing with the sound of breakers crashing over the infamous shoals to the south.

The station was located at the tip of the legendary Outer Banks, on what one early map called the "Promontorium Tremendum" (horrible headland). From here the shoals extend seaward some ten miles, separating North Carolina's Onslow and Raleigh Bays, and snaring the occasional seafarer who ventures too close.

As dawn broke to reveal an overcast day of ominous gray, the cook completed his preparations and passed the word to the surfman on night watch that he could call the others. The station's keeper, Fred Gilliken, and his crew of seven slept in quarters on the second deck of the white, two-story building with its distinctive, sharply pitched, red roof, topped by a lookout's cupola.

Responding to the breakfast call, Bos'n Yeomans, the station's number-one surfman and second in command, turned from dressing to observe the day, and the churning sea to the south. He was startled to see the unmistakable outline of a ship with its sail being furled, lying in the surf near the heart of the shoals.

As he sounded the alarm, Surfman Yeomans and Keeper Gilliken ran to the small lookout tower atop the station. Through long glasses they were able to see more clearly. A three-masted schooner of nearly 400 tons was surrounded by boiling surf. She was of a type which frequently sought a lee in Cape Lookout Bight, behind the station. Famous as a rendezvous for such pirates as Blackbeard, the Bight often served as anchorage for twenty or more vessels.

It appeared to Keeper Gilliken that the vessel had sailed into the shoals from the south, running before the wind and then broaching in the strong, erratic currents which predominate off Cape Point. The schooner's still furling sail indicated that she had probably grounded only a short time earlier, just before dawn. Seas broke over the ship as she lay firmly in the grip of the shoal's shifting sands.

Ignoring the temptation of a hot breakfast, the Coast Guardsmen rushed from the station, pulling on foul-weather clothing as they ran, and began the half-mile trot to the protecting bight where their motor lifeboat was moored. Preparing the boat for the job ahead and wishing fervently that the grounding had occurred closer to shore, where a breeches buoy could be used, Keeper Gilliken's thoughts turned to another rescue.

Several years earlier the American salt carrier *Melrose*, off course in the face of another sou'easter, had run ashore a short distance to the north, on Core Banks. Gilliken then had been the number-one surfman at Core Banks Station.

The surf had been too rough for a boat, he recalled. So, he and the crew fired a line over the breakers with the station's Lyle gun. Once the

CWO Freddie Gilliken recalled the first rescue he performed as a Coast Guardsman. Photo courtesy of the Cape Lookout National Seashore.

messenger line had been shot aboard the schooner, the endless whip line with a tail block and an instruction board had been sent over. A three-inch line was then secured to the whip line and fed across the 150 yards of raging surf, to be secured above the tail block. The block and lines had then been made fast to a crosstree on the mast of the *Melrose*.

Since the ship had grounded midway between Core Banks and Portsmouth Island Stations, some twenty miles apart, the crews of the two stations had joined forces. Together, they had set up a portable tripod [crotch] under the hawser, and buried a sand anchor to hold the block and tackle which would keep the hawser tight. The breeches buoy, consisting of a ring life buoy supporting a pair of short canvas pants (breeches) was then suspended from a traveling pulley that could be drawn back and forth along the three-inch hawser.

Gilliken vividly recalled the attempt of the first *Melrose* crewman to enter the breeches buoy. The tail block had been secured to the mast with too much slack; the buoy could not be pulled close enough to the crosstree for boarding.

After repeated unsuccessful attempts from the shore to signal the *Melrose* crew to shorten the block, the Core Banks' keeper had directed Surfman Gilliken to get into the buoy, ride it to the *Melrose*, shorten the whip, and start sending the crew ashore. With the skeptical encouragement of his fellow lifesavers, Gilliken recollected, he had willingly entered the swinging buoy and rocked across the tumult of water to the mast of the salt carrier.

Once over the ship, the buoy again stopped several feet from the mast. Gilliken had to draw himself up out of the breeches and pull himself across the remaining distance hand-over-hand while dangling from the hawser. He remembered how the sea had seemed to pound the wreck some fifty feet below with increased fury, as if trying to knock him from the line. But years of launching and rowing surfboats had kept Gilliken's short, slight body in shape for the hazardous task.

Once safely to the mast, Gilliken had resecured the tail block and lowered himself through the rigging to the schooner's deck. He had collected the frightened crew and instructed them in how to get into the buoy. He then saw each person safely ashore before making his own escape.

But now there would be no breeches buoy; nor would there be anyone to advise him on what actions to take. At thirty-seven, Gilliken had a lifetime of familiarity with the sea and eleven years of experience as a member of the Life-Saving Service, which had become the Coast Guard only two months earlier. Upon leaving Core Banks the year before, he had been named Keeper of Cape Lookout Station. Rescue responsibility and decisions would be all his today.

As he ordered the engine of his motorized lifeboat brought to life and the lines cast off, Keeper Fred Gilliken's trained eye scanned the boat that would carry him and his crew into the storm. Everything must be secured before they rounded the spit and met the full fury of the storm.

The boat was a "good, able craft," in Gilliken's view, highly regarded for routine assistance work. It was 36 feet in length and among the first power-driven boats acquired by the Life-Saving Service. A pioneer in lifeboat design, it was equipped with a Holmes engine, featured a heavy lead keel to facilitate righting, and had a self-bailing capability. These features would become standard on the Coast Guard lifeboats for decades to follow. Its hull was of double diagonal wooden planking. A single, hinged mast amidship (power still not completely trusted) and a canopy-covered coxswain's station completed the boat's lines.

Watching the sturdy lifeboat make her way across the sheltered bight, fishermen at anchor could see the Cape Lookout crew busily donning life jackets and stringing additional life lines. Later the fishermen would tell the Coast Guardsmen that they never expected to see crew or boat return from the raging seas.

Underway at 0645, less than an hour after Surfman Yeoman's sighting, the Coast Guard crew needed several hours to work their way to the strickened schooner. Struggling against an icy March wind estimated in excess of forty knots, and seas approaching twenty feet, the small boat shook free of wave after crashing wave as it alternated between being submerged and tossed skyward. The crew, combating a chill factor of well below zero, fought to keep warm, and to hold on.

By midmorning, Gilliken had brought the rescuers to a point near the wreck, just off the shoal. With occasional glimpses of the shore, he estimated his position to be "abeam of Blue Fish Lump," a popular fishing spot during calmer weather. Now it was the resting place of the *Sylvia C. Hall.*

Observing the schooner's nameboard, the Coast Guardsmen also could see the waves pounding against her sides with such intensity that sheets of spray and foam were sent flying over her crosstrees. Later they would learn that she was carrying a cargo of lumber from Jacksonville, Florida to New York.

The schooner lay in the center of the breaking surf on an easterly heading with a broken lifeboat trailing from her port side. The currents and uneven shoals worked the seas against the wind so that surf could be seen breaking from all directions.

Studying the surf and floating wreckage, Gilliken ordered Yeomans, who was at the helm, to begin a slow approach to the wreck while Gilliken attempted to point out a safe path between the more dangerous parts of the shoal. But just as they entered the breakers, a giant wave broke over them from astern, pounding down with tons of force. Two of the crew were knocked from their seats, saved from going overboard by the extra lines rigged earlier. Tyra Moore, one of those thrown to the deck, received an injury to his hip. His considerable pain suggested that it had been broken.

The only damage to the boat was the loss of the coxswain's canopy. The boat's self-bailing features carried off the unwelcome water. The rescue attempt continued. Then, another giant wave broke, flooding the engine compartment. The engine quit! Powerless, the Coast Guardsmen realized that they were at the mercy of the storm, and soon to join the *Sylvia C. Hall.*

With lightning speed, Gilliken grabbed the helm, working it feverishly to keep the boat from broaching. Yeomans grasped the starting crank and began to whirl it with all his strength. The engineer, Del Mason,

This rare photo shows the door to the boathouse of the Cape Lookout (NC) Life-Saving Station. The year that the Life-Saving Service and Revenue Cutter Service formed the Coast Guard (1915), the new organization built a new station at Cape Lookout. United States Coast Guard photo.

disappeared into the compartment to see what he could do, but not before entreating his shipmates to watch out for him should the boat capsize. Then, as quickly as it had stopped, the engine caught, allowing Gilliken to bring the boat around smartly to meet the seas head on.

Thwarted in their initial attempt by the storm's overwhelming strength, the lifesavers withdrew from the shoal to attend to the injured Moore and the uncertain engine. From a point well clear of the surfline, the Cape Lookout crew spent the remainder of the day clawing into the seas and trying to correct the erratic performance of the wet engine. Moore was found to have no definite broken bones, but a severely painful bruise and possible fracture. Hunger and a wet, cold numbness added to his misery and that of his companions.

As darkness started to claim the bleak March sky, the storm continued unabated. Keeper Gilliken realized there was little he could do. Engineer Mason continued to worry over the engine's performance. A low fuel state was also becoming a concern. With great reluctance, Gilliken directed the crew to return to the station for food, fuel, dry clothing, and rest. The constant effort to "just hang on" for hours on end had taken its toll. Turning his injured lifeboat homeward, the keeper could imagine the fear and faltering hope which the crew of the *Sylvia C. Hall* were experiencing. The captain of the *Hall* would tell him later that it was "a bad sight!"

While their departure was viewed with trepidation on the wreck, the Lookout crew's return was cause for much relief among the waiting fishermen. They had lost sight of the lifeboat soon after it had rounded the spit and dived into the building seas. Concerned that the Coast Guardsmen be "destroyed," the fishing fleet had sent out a search boat, only to have it turned back.

During the night the rescuers' luck took a favorable turn. The storm began to moderate. Yet, Keeper Gilliken would leave nothing to chance. If the *Sylvia C. Hall* crew were still alive, a question which haunted the surfmen all night, they were determined to bring them safely ashore. With this in mind, the Coast Guardsmen mustered at the boathouse before dawn on Thursday the 18th. Assisted by the station's horse, the crew hauled a 26-foot pulling surfboat to the bight for launching. The Cape Lookout crew would take both of their boats for this second attempt.

Expecting little change in sea conditions, Gilliken and Yeomans developed a plan whereby the motor lifeboat with two men aboard would act as a backup, while the pulling surfboat, with its reliable "Norwegian steam" (muscle power), would make the rescue. Remembering the experience of the previous day, they did not want the larger, more vulnerable 36-footer to chance a trip into the surf unless absolutely necessary. Further, if the seas were as rough as expected, she would not be able to go alongside the wreck to take off crew. They would have to come off from the jib boom. This would require dropping the mast on the 36-footer.

The anxious Coast Guard crew, divided between the two surfboats, departed promptly at dawn. Only the cook was left ashore. Even the badly limping Moore refused to stay behind, and took his place in the pulling boat.

With Surfman John Lewis and Engineer Mason as crew, the motor lifeboat once again rounded the spit and headed toward the shoal; the pulling boat towed astern. While the wind had diminished considerably, the seas had moderated only slightly. The temperature remained bitingly cold. Thus, the trip was nearly as unpleasant as that of the previous day.

As the two lifeboats approached the *Hall*, Gilliken could see with considerable relief that the wreck, though badly beaten, was still intact. The chances of the crews having survived the night were good.

Nearing the surf line, Gilliken ordered the towline cast off, and the crew of the pulling boat laid to their oars. They successfully navigated the surf that had nearly trapped them the day before, and moved close aboard the *Hall*. Rigging and debris were everywhere. It was apparent to the pulling boat crew that the rescue would have to be their rescue. It would be particularly dangerous for the motor surfer to maneuver among the many entanglements.

The Coast Guardsmen yelled to the men on deck to rig a line from the jib boom and lower themselves into the 26-footer, clear of the wreck. Two haggard survivors succeeded in reaching the pulling boat in this manner, as Gilliken attempted to maintain the boat's precarious position against the surf. However, he was soon forced to order the surfmen to pull clear. A freshening of the wind and a building of the seas made it too dangerous to remain alongside.

Upon clearing the surf, Gilliken learned that there were three more aboard the wreck, including the captain. Allowing his men to regain their strength, Gilliken patiently watched the seas, waiting for an opportunity to re-enter the shoals. Then, as the storm began to show signs of exhaustion, he saw his chance. During a momentary lull, he headed the pulling boat back into the deadly breakers.

Having seen the Coast Guard come and go without them twice before, the remaining *Hall* crew in quick succession executed the climb onto the boom and the heart-stopping drop into the surfboat. The surfmen were thankful for the rapid exodus as they called upon their last reserves of strength to maintain position and pull out. But the former Life-Saving Servicemen's satisfaction in knowing that they had just saved all hands in their first rescue as Coast Guardsmen made the trip home all the easier. Their only regret was that they had not been able to save the shipwrecked crew's belongings.

Sixty years later, Chief Warrant Officer Fred Gilliken looked back on the *Sylvia C. Hall* as the most dangerous and demanding rescue of his forty years in the Life-Saving Service and Coast Guard. With unmistakable pride, he also recalled that this was the first rescue of a shipwrecked crew in North Carolina under the newly created Coast Guard.

Regardless of the name, Life-Saving Service or Coast Guard, "Captain" Fred Gilliken remembered that his crew was "Semper Paratus," always ready.

Crossing the Line: The Story of Ocean City's Jack Jernee

by Fred Miller
(Volume 8, Issue 2)

The Ocean City Beach Patrol traces its roots to 1871, the year the United States Life-Saving Service erected three stations on the eight-mile long barrier island then called Peck's Beach.

The men of the Life-Saving Service patrolled the desolate beach often risking their lives to save the lives of those in peril from shipwrecks.

Each station had a captain and a crew of at least six men who were experienced at handling lifeboats in rough surf. They were on duty from September 1 to May 1 of each year.

During the calm summer months their services weren't needed, so many lifesavers spent their days in front of hotels and bathhouses saving drowning bathers in return for donations.

By 1900, the three original stations had been replaced with large modern buildings located at 4th Street, 36th Street, and 58th Street, and the City of Ocean City was paying men to protect bathers.

Jack G. Jernee-the father of professional lifeguarding in Ocean City-was a member of the U. S. Life-Saving Service.

In 1913, he was assigned to the 4th Street station and from then on he considered Ocean City his home. He served in the Coast Guard during World War I. In 1920, Mayor Joseph G. Champion hired him to be the captain of the Ocean City lifeguards.

Jernee immediately began calling the squad the Ocean City Beach Patrol. He led the growing life-saving squad for 22 years and under his leadership the OCBP became nationally recognized for its life-saving skills (no drownings on a lifeguard protected beach), athletic prowess (National Lifeguard Champions in 1933, 1934 and 1935), giant water shows, and flag ceremonies held each day at the Music Pier.

Captain Jack Jernee repairs his "easy to operate, practically indestructible, and approved after the most severe tests" can buoy. Photo courtesy of Fred Miller.

Captain Jernee attributed his success to the many lifeguards who had been members of the Life-Saving Service and Coast Guard. Their knowledge of the different codes and their experience with the sea prepared them for the Ocean City Beach Patrol.

Mayor Harry Headley appointed him chief of police in 1933 and for three years Jernee headed both public safety departments.

"Beach Patrol Chief In Navy On Monday" was the headline on the front page of the July 16, 1942, issue of the Ocean City Sentinel-Ledger. The article began, "Jack G. Jernee, who has been captain of the Ocean City Beach Patrol for the past 22 years, will leave Monday to join the U. S. Navy for the duration, it was disclosed yesterday. He applied for a commission and has been accepted for active duty, to report next Monday with the rank of Warrant Officer." Jernee was 49 years old when he joined the Navy.

When World War II ended, Jernee returned to Ocean City and bought the former U. S. Life-Saving station at 36th Street and opened the Ocean City Academy, a summer camp with a nautical atmosphere for boys 12 to 18 years old. The camp operated until 1949 when it became a hotel called Jernee Manor.

Jernee died on January 19, 1975 at the age of 82. The lifeguards dedicated their 1975 yearbook to him saying, "During his years as Captain, the Ocean City Beach Patrol became famous as one of the most efficient life saving units in the United States."

The Great Rum War on Long Island

by Van R. Field
(Volume 4, Issue 4)

The character of the newly formed U.S. Coast Guard was being shaped after World War I, "the war to end all wars." The climate of the country was that of turmoil. Thousands of American troops were brought home from the battlefields of Europe, deloused, paraded in public, and mustered out of service, leaving large numbers of men looking for jobs. There was no G.I. Bill in 1918 to ease their way into civilian life.

City people were pitted against country people, representatives of diverse cultures looking at their rapidly changing society from either side of a widening gap. There were many problems, some of them sound surprisingly modern. The Ku Klux Klan became an evil force, more in rural areas than in the cities. There was a fear of the recent Bolshevik Revolution spreading to the U.S. from Russia.

Fundamentalists from rural areas stirred up hatreds. They, along with the Women's Christian Temperance Union and the Anti-Saloon League, managed to influence the Congress to pass the Volstead Act, providing the enforcement apparatus for the 18th Amendment, which prohibited the sale of intoxicating beverages. On January 16, 1920, that act became the law of the land, the same year that women won their right to vote.

From start to finish, prohibition was a disaster. Drinking increased among young men and women. Contempt for the law was widespread. Prohibition actually encouraged the very evils that it was meant to destroy. Women cast off their Victorian clothing and mores. Short skirts, bobbed hair and lipstick were seen on young women both on the streets and in the speakeasies where they danced to the new jazz.

America went into World War I a nation of the 19th century. After the war, convulsed into the 20th century, with changes in lifestyle that included radio broadcasts delivered directly into the home, and cars in every driveway.

Into this mix, the new Coast Guard was thrust suddenly into the role of enforcing the smuggling law and stopping the flow of liquor into the country. Bootlegging gave organized crime an instant profitable business. Congress had made no plans to hire more customs agents to enforce this new act. Now that liquor was illegal, drinking became the "in" thing to do. When the police, who usually looked the other way, did bring someone in, the judges usually threw the case out. Coast Guardsmen at this point were paid less than their Life-Saving Service predecessors. Honest jobs were hard to come by, but the easy money that came with the bootlegging reached almost everyone along the coastal areas of the country.

During Prohibition, Long Island, New York was a broad highway - from Montauk to Manhattan - over which trucks, cars, and anything else that would roll were headed westward toward the city with their distilled spirits and wines. Just about every creek, dock, or landing area of any sort was used at one time or another to land illicit liquor. Ships from Europe and Canada hung out offshore in international waters. Anything that floated was used to transport the liquid cargo from the mother ships to trucks waiting ashore, from speedboats with large engines designed for the purpose down to craft under sail. Sometimes large private yachts, normally painted white, were spotted with telltale black scratches in their fine paint, indicating that they had been alongside a large ship.

The only inlets that passed the barrier beaches on the south shore of Long Island in the Twenties were, from west to east, Rockaway Beach, Jones Beach and Fire Island. In 1931, shortly before the end of Prohibition, the Moriches Inlet broke through right between the Moriches Coast Guard Station and the remains of the wreck of the sidewheeler Franklin.

Fishermen loaded up with their illegal cargo at mother ships resting outside the Coast Guard's three-mile jurisdictional limit, in a line-up known as Rum Row. They then landed the booze on shore with their fishing dories.

From there it was transported to waiting boats on Great South Bay and to docks on the mainland, to be unloaded into waiting trucks, for the final leg of the journey to the local speakeasies or the big city.

The frame of the engine of the Franklin, wrecked in 1854, loomed several feet out of the water less than a mile from the Coast Guard station. The bootleggers had rigged an endless clothesline-like pulley arrangement between the wreck and the shore a hundred yards or so away. Dories would tie up to the wreck and run the booze in to the waiting crew ashore, thus escaping the necessity of a surf landing with their precious cargo.

What happened to the liquor after it was landed was related to the writer as follows: "A fishing boat would pull into the public dock at the foot of Bay Avenue in Eastport, Long Island, and unload cases of booze directly into a 'borrowed' U.S. mail truck. The driver was handed a bunch of envelopes with numbers on them. As he went on his rounds he would be stopped at police checkpoints. An envelope was handed over and he was allowed to proceed. This was continued until all the cases of liquor were delivered. Just about everyone was paid off."

In this climate it was no wonder that some of the local surfmen developed cases of "night blindness." There were stories of Coast Guard surfboats being used to deliver the illegal cargo. The State Police were often on hand ashore to make sure that the illegal liquor was not hijacked by a rival gang.

As the war escalated, the Coast Guard had fast boats built in local shipyards around Freeport, Long Island. The bootleggers would have theirs built at the same yards, with the proviso that they received the faster boats.

It was estimated in 1924 that the Coast Guard was stopping only about 5% of the total influx of liquor from all the neighboring countries and Europe. Over time the Coast Guard obtained some of the vessels they had seized from rumrunners, to use against them. Usually seized vessels were sold at government auction and bought back by the folks who originally owned them. Congressional action also resulted in the Coast Guard receiving twenty destroyers, two minesweepers, and some smaller boats from the U.S. Navy. In addition, money was appropriated to build 323 small, fast boats. With this new fleet, the Coast Guard engaged in many battles.

Attempts to board suspected rumrunners often resulted in chases, with the Coast Guard throwing several shells across the bows of rummies. If this tactic did not work, they attempted to disable the vessels by gunfire. Occasionally, casualties resulted.

One December day in 1929, Boatswain Alexander Cornell finished his patrol of Gardiner's Bay on the east end of Long Island aboard the *CG-290*, a 75-foot cutter (or "six-bitter") built specifically to stop rumrunners, anchoring near the entrance of Shelter Island Sound just north of Noyac Bay. The vessel was hard to spot against the black shoreline. After only an hour's wait, a vessel approached with no lights showing. The *CG-290* weighed anchor and as the darkened vessel passed, it went in pursuit at full throttle. The patrol boat pulled alongside, ordering the other vessel to halt. As the vessels came together, the *CG-290* split a wooden railing on the other vessel. The suspected rummy was ordered to drop its anchor.

Captain O. Nelson identified his vessel as the *Beatrice K* out of Gloucester, Massachusetts. He produced papers that included a license for mackerel and cod fishing. While two Coast Guardsmen searched his boat, Nelson decided to act friendly and talked to Boatswain Cornell. He told of being boarded by the destroyer Fanning and receiving a clean bill of health after a thorough search. Nelson claimed that he had 60,000 pounds of fish aboard for New York and that they would spoil if he were detained. He said that his generator had broken down and his batteries were dead, which was the reason he was running without lights, and that the *Beatrice K* was leaking badly. He claimed to be a stranger to the area and had picked Sag Harbor as a likely place for repairs. Further conversation, though, revealed that he had been fishing off George's Bank for fifteen years. The men searching the boat's hold said that it indeed contained fish and ice.

Cornell thought things over, and to him some things did not ring quite true. No liquor had been found, but why would a ship needing repairs go twenty miles out of its way while passing up the facilities available at New Bedford, Newport or New London, all of which were on the way from the fishing grounds to Sag Harbor? The batteries were found to be completely dry, indicating that they had been dumped out. When asked why there was a bucket over the exhaust the captain became angry and threw the bucket over the side, but he didn't seem to mind the split

Among the vessels utilized by the Coast Guard in its war on demon rum during Prohibition was the 75-foot Patrol Boat, or "Six-Bitter," like the CG-222, *built by the Vineyard Shipbuilding Company of Milford, Delaware in 1925, and eventually sold to the United States Navy on March 27, 1934. United States Coast Guard photo from the collection of William D. Wilkinson.*

rail. Cornell could not believe that someone fishing George's Banks for a decade and a half would be so unfamiliar with Long Island Sound. Acting on his suspicions, Cornell decided that the vessel needed to be searched more thoroughly. Placing a man aboard, he ordered the *Beatrice K* to proceed to New London.

At Section Base Four her holds were opened, the fish and ice removed. About eighteen inches down there was a layer of tarpaper, and under it was discovered 1600 sacks of Meadville Pure Rye Whiskey! Once the booze was found and Cornell addressed Nelson as "Captain," Nelson replied, "Don't call me captain, I am not the captain. He left in a dory before you came on board." The crew was arrested and the vessel was seized for probable cause. Cornell received a commendation from the base commander and a Commandant's Letter of Commendation for his actions.

This seemingly watertight case went to trial. Surprisingly, the Judge held that the Coast Guard had no right to arrest the crew of the *Beatrice K* for running without lights and no right to search the vessel without a search warrant. He agreed with the defense attorneys that the vessel was the "home" of the crewmembers and was inviolable for the purpose of an extensive search! The *Beatrice K* was released on bond and the crew found not guilty. It was a ridiculous ruling but it stood. This aroused the indignation of Coast Guardsmen far and wide, as it set an unsavory precedent that could be used to obtain the release of other vessels that might be seized in the future.

Later that month, on December 28, 1929, Boatswain Cornell was again underway on the *CG-290*, leaving the New London base for a joint patrol in the eastern passage of Narragansett Bay with the *CG-241*. Their intention was to prevent any smuggling vessel from entering the area. The skipper of the *CG-290* had over sixteen years of sea experience in the Merchant Marine and the Navy as well as the Coast Guard.

CG-290 took up a position near Dumpling Rock that evening, with *CG-241* on the other side of the channel near Fort Adams in Newport. Meanwhile the *Black Duck*, a speedboat-type rumrunner, had taken on a load of 383 bags of assorted liquor from the British ship *Symor* and was headed into Narragansett Bay. The "black," as rumrunners were called, was heard faintly at 2:15 a.m. The sea was calm and a patchy fog present. Under these conditions sounds traveled well.

The *Black Duck* had two 300-horsepower engines, was heavily muffled, and was equipped with a smoke screen device. It was very fast and had eluded Cornell for over a year. As Cornell peered intently into the night, the speedboat suddenly appeared out of the mist moving at high speed without lights. Cornell turned his searchlight on the vessel, instantly recognizing it. Some of the cargo was plainly visible on the deck. He swung his searchlight alternating towards the boat and his own vessel's Coast Guard ensign, at the same time sounding his klaxon horn as a signal for the speedboat to stop. The *Black Duck* passed within seventy-five feet of the bow of the *CG-290*, and as it slid by, Cornell used his loudhailer in another attempt to call it to a halt. No one was visible on the decks. As the rumrunner was drawing away, Cornell ordered the seaman at the machine gun to open fire. He did so, aiming for the stern of the boat, as was the standard operating procedure in such cases. His burst consisted of twenty-one shots in about three seconds. At the same time, the *Black Duck* swerved sharply to the left with the result that the shots raked the port side of the vessel and hit the pilot house instead of going harmlessly astern. Then the gun jammed and the *Black Duck* disappeared toward shore.

Shortly thereafter, the black reappeared out of the fog heading for the *CG-290*. It turned on its lights and maneuvered with difficulty next to the Coast Guard boat. The black was then secured to the *CG-290* and boarded. They found one man crumpled up on deck near the wheel and two more on the deck of the pilothouse, all dead. A fourth man, wounded in the hand, was given first aid. *CG-290*, after taking one sack of liquor aboard as evidence, proceeded to Fort Adams with the *Black Duck* in tow.

A Coast Guard Board of Investigation cleared Cornell and his gunner of any possible wrongdoing in the case of the deaths of the three men aboard the *Black Duck*, as later did a special grand jury in Providence, Rhode Island. The *Black Duck* was turned over to the Coast Guard and became *CG-808*, now on the other side of the Rum War. The public, however, were not so forgiving. A short time later a protesting mob tore down recruiting posters in Boston. In New London, a gang brutally beat up two Coast Guardsmen, resulting in fines for three of the attackers.

In the end, only repealing Prohibition solved the problems that the law itself had caused. When you see an old timer at your local marina. You might just go up to him and ask about the rum running days. Most of the participants are now gone, but the stories remain. After Prohibition was officially repealed on December 5, 1933, through the passing of the 21st Amendment to the Constitution, the subject became taboo. Not many liked to talk of the "old days" because it simply involved friends, relatives, and neighbors fighting back against what they saw as an unjust law.

Powerless: The Wreck of the Robert E. Lee

by John J. Galluzzo

(Volume 5, Issue 4)

Composer George Gershwin sailed for Europe on March 9, 1928, to perform his "Rhapsody in Blue" for that continent's classical music devotees for the first time. That same day, boxer George "The Saginaw Kid" Lavigne, the world's second lightweight champion under the Marques of Queensbury rules, heard the ring bell toll for the last time, dying at the age of fifty-nine. And in a landmark decision, a U.S. Circuit Court judge ruled that Native Americans should not be held accountable to U.S. naturalization laws and should be allowed to cross the American and Canadian borders at will, as recognized by the Jay Treaty of 1796.

These news stories would be lost on the people of Plymouth, Massachusetts, pushed to the back pages of the newspapers by an unexpected and unnecessary local tragedy.

Plymouth, tucked away on the western shore of Cape Cod Bay, lays claim to the title "America's Hometown," the site where Elder William Brewster, Captain Myles Standish, Governor William Bradford and the rest of the Pilgrims set up the first permanent non-indigenous settlement in the New World. And although hidden as it was by the outer arm of Cape Cod, the harbor at Plymouth, protected to the northeast by a natural breakwater known as the Gurnet, became an important and active port over the next century and a half.

The fleet of whalers, coasters, smacks and packets that called Plymouth Harbor home was nearly decimated by the British during the American Revolution. By 1807 the fleet had regained its strength, but President Thomas Jefferson's Embargo Act of December of that year, forbidding

American ships from trading with foreign nations, forced many of those ships to rest at anchor for fourteen months. Only around 1820 did Plymouth's mariners once again begin to profit from their life's work.

The true growth of the harbor, though, began in 1824 with the opening of the Plymouth Cordage Company. In 1810 America boasted 173 ropewalks. Rope made the maritime world of the early nineteenth century move just as much as wood or sailcloth.

"Nothing symbolic of the sea would be complete without a piece of rope," writes Frederick William Wallace in The Romance of Rope in 1932. "It has bound the world together. It is enshrined in the sailor's heart because the cast-off mooring line is the last link with the land - last to leave and the first to go ashore." The constant flow of raw materials to the Plymouth Cordage Company when coupled with the goods needed for other local iron and textile factories made Plymouth Harbor one of the busiest spots in New England by the late nineteenth century. By 1899, Plymouth was supplying one-seventh of all the cordage in the world.

General Superintendent Sumner Kimball and the United States Life-Saving Service recognized the importance of the mercantile interests of Plymouth Harbor to the nation soon after the service's 1871 rebirth, beginning construction of two stations to protect the harbor just two years later. The Gurnet station, four and a half miles to the northeast of the town, stood at the southern end of the narrow peninsula that reached from the town of Duxbury to the north to the mouth of Plymouth Harbor. The station shared the end of the peninsula with the twin Gurnet Lighthouses, home to the first female lightkeeper in America, Hannah Thomas. Six and a half miles to the southeast the service constructed another 1874-type station on Manomet Point.

Both early structures served the local mariners well, but time, the elements, and the expansion of the service's workforce and duties called for the older simple lifeboat stations to be replaced with modern facilities. A Bibb #2-type station replaced the boathouse at the Gurnet in 1892, while a Duluth-type station supplanted the Manomet Point building in 1901. In both instances the older stations remained in use as auxiliary structures to the main buildings.

Because of its positioning on a high cliff and its proximity to that cliff's edge, the new Manomet Point station had a peculiarity all its own. The boat room doors that would normally be prominent on the front of the

Lifeboats stand by the stranded Robert E. Lee. *Photo courtesy of the Old Colony Club.*

building instead were placed on the inland side of the station, to protect the surfmen from tumbling over the cliff with their equipment in the adrenaline-pumping frenzy of the first few moments of a rescue effort.

A decade later a significant public works project changed maritime traffic patterns off that town forever. The opening of the Cape Cod Canal on July 29, 1914, meant that ships that had for nearly three centuries rounded Cape Cod to reach Plymouth and Boston could now sail under the protection of the Cape itself and bypass the waters off the Great Beach. For Plymouth, though, the change had come too late. Many of the industries that had made the town strong had failed, although the foresight of the proprietors of the Plymouth Cordage Company who skillfully sought new markets for the products in the wheat and oil fields as American shipping changed from sail to steam kept that particular business alive. Nevertheless, easier access to Plymouth Harbor from the south did not spur an economic upturn for the town. The surfmen and keepers at Manomet Point and the Gurnet, and, eventually, the crew of the auxiliary station built at the eastern end of the Cape Cod Canal in 1919, now stood watch over a parade of ships passing by offshore, most of which would never fall prey to the dangers of the harbor's channels.

Somewhat symbolically, the first ship to pass through the Cape Cod Canal, the Hull to Boston steamer *Rose Standish*, was captained by Osceola James, the son of famous lifesaver Joshua James.

The 400-foot, 5284-ton New York to Boston steamer *Robert E. Lee* was headed north after passing through the Cape Cod Canal in near blizzard conditions on the evening of March 9, 1928. Snow, sleet and hail, some of which entered the wheelhouse driven by forty-five mile per hour winds, hindered Captain Harland W. Robinson's ability to navigate his ship. The thick atmosphere shrouded the twin fourth order Fresnel lenses seven miles north at the Gurnet, aids intended to help mariners steer clear of the dangerous Mary Ann Rocks. Without their help, Robinson was in trouble.

The *Robert E. Lee* missed the first set of rocks, but struck and ran hard aground on the second. The vessel began to ship water on its starboard side, and Robinson ordered the seacocks opened, settling the *Lee*, and then sent out an immediate SOS distress call. At midnight, with high tide just two hours away, he feared for the safety of his passengers and crew. But the stranding had been so relatively gentle that some of the 273 passengers slept through the entire incident.

Ashore, Boatswain's Mate William Cashman and the Coast Guard crew at Manomet Point attempted to contact the stranded steamer by flashing light for over an hour. But the fog that had settled in rose and fell in such a pattern that it made communication impossible.

Feeling unsure of the situation, Cashman called his men to the station's pulling surfboat. After several attempts at launching their vessel in the pounding surf in the darkness, they opted to wait for sunrise. After the turn of the tide, the *Lee* stabilized, and some of the passengers took to singing songs to pass the time. When the sun rose, one man awoke and headed for the onboard barber's shop for a shave, unaware of what had transpired during the night.

At first light, Cashman and his crew - Frank Griswold, Edward Stark, Alden Proctor, Irving Wood, Joseph Ducharme, and a local mechanic named Ernest Douglas who volunteered to go out in place of Arthur Young, who was sick at home in Orleans - launched the surfboat onto the still-churning seas and headed for the *Lee*.

The 125-foot patrol boat *Bonham* had arrived on scene during the night, as had the Coast Guard destroyer *Paulding* and the 178-foot cutter

Although the U.S. Life-Saving Service had begun experimenting with powered lifeboats as early as 1899, the crew of the Manomet Point Coast Guard Station in Plymouth, Massachusetts, responded to the stranded steamer Robert E. Lee *on the morning of March 10, 1928, in a pulling surfboat. Photo courtesy of the Old Colony Club of Plymouth.*

Tuscarora. The 125-foot patrol boat *Active* and the 75-foot patrol boat *CG176* stood by as well. Cashman climbed aboard *Lee* and talked with the ship's captain about the alternatives for removing the passengers and crew to safety. Both agreed that rowing them to shore in the surfboat would be a long, tedious process, and that shuttling the passengers to the larger vessels would be their best course of action. The Coast Guard had also dispatched two 36-foot motor lifeboats during the night, one from the Wood End station in Provincetown at the end of the Cape Cod peninsula and one from the auxiliary station at the Cape Cod Canal to the scene. Once the first transfer had been made, just after 11 a.m., Cashman and his crew headed for shore, confident that the situation had been correctly tended to. By the end of the day, every person on the ship would be safe on dry land.

As the Manomet Point crew approached the shoreline, though, tragedy struck. A wave, described by one of the Coast Guardsmen as twenty-five feet in height, lifted the stern of the craft, jamming the bow into the seafloor, pitchpoling it onto the top of the crew. The seven stunned men floated helplessly in the water, shocked and injured from the vessel's unexpected overturning. Two hundred spectators watched on shore as Surfman Griswold momentarily surfaced, and then sank out of sight. Boatswain's Mate Cashman clung to an oar as Surfman Stark complained to his friends Proctor, Ducharme and Wood that he had severe pain around his heart. Wood, who believed that the gunwale had struck Proctor when the boat flipped, helped push him onto the overturned vessel.

Local residents Russell Anderson, Earl Harper and Massachusetts state trooper John Horgan scrambled to the shoreline where they found a leaky dory. Cutting it loose, they rowed toward the drowning men. From around the point lobstermen Harry F. Eddy and friend Daniel Sullivan rowed another dory to the scene, Anderson and crew pulled Cashman, Proctor, and Wood into their boat while Eddy and Sullivan grabbed Stark and Ducharme to safety. Civilian Douglas told them "I can hang on. Take someone else first." Griswold could not be located.

The Wood End 36-foot motor lifeboat arrived on the scene and transferred Proctor, Douglas, Wood and Stark to the *Paulding*, which headed for the Chelsea Naval Hospital in Boston. Ducharme and Sampson were taken to Plymouth's Jordan Hospital. Twenty-seven year old Edward Stark died in transit.

On the beach, doctor Edgar Hill and Fire Chief Albert E. Hiller worked on the unconscious form of Boatswain's Mate William Cashman for a little more than two hours before pronouncing him dead. A priest on the scene performed the last rites. Surfman Frank Griswold's body washed ashore a day later.

In the days that followed the tragedy, as 10,000 sightseers packed the roads leading to Manomet Point, the people of Plymouth looked for answers to seemingly simple questions. Why had the federal government allowed the men charged with protecting the coast to work in a building with no toilets, heated by coal stoves and lit only by kerosene lamps? Why should there not be a lighthouse erected on Manomet Point to steer ships away from the Mary Ann Rocks? And why, nearly three decades after the introduction of the service's first motor lifeboats, were these men manually rowing to the scene of a rescue? In the end, the locals surmised, the Coast Guardsmen of Manomet Point had been left powerless to save their own lives.

Two months after the disaster, the people of Plymouth gathered outside the Manomet Point station to dedicate a simple memorial to the fallen Coast Guardsmen. Dedicated on May 30, 1928, to the memories of Boatswain's Mate William E. Cashman, Surfman Frank W. Griswold, and Surfman Edward P. Stark, the plaque on the stone reads in part, "Greater love hath no man than this, that a man lay down his life for his friends," the same Biblical passage carved onto the grave marker of Joshua James, and an all-too familiar reminder of the deadly risks taken by America's lifesavers when mariners are in distress at sea.

Ordeal In The Ice: The 1936 Rescue At The Charlevoix, Michigan Coast Guard Station

by Geoffrey D. Reynolds

(Volume 6, Issue 1)

On Saturday, February 8, 1936, Boatswain's Mate Earl Cunningham interrupted his day off to come to the aid of fishermen Claude Beardsley and Beardsley's son-in-law, Clayton Brown, after the ice they were fishing from broke loose and moved out into a Lake Michigan blizzard. Little did Cunningham know that he would lose his life in the rescue. Cunningham's death was the only loss of personnel from the Charlevoix, Michigan station in over 100 years.

Earl Cunningham was born December 16, 1895, in Kinde, Huron County, Michigan. He was one of five children born to George and Annie Cunningham. He spent his childhood on the family farm in Afton, Michigan.

When war in Europe erupted, Cunningham enlisted on June 24, 1918 as a private in the American Expeditionary Forces of the United States Army, seeing action in France and Germany. He was mustered out of the service as a corporal in August 1919 and returned to Afton to work at the Campbell Stone Company, eventually learning to operate the Vulcan locomotive and the steam shovel for the company. After marrying his sweetheart, Miss Helen Teatro, in 1921, Cunningham settled into married life. The couple's family began in 1925 with their first son, Richard, followed by two more boys, Hubert and Wayne, born in 1929 and 1930 respectively.

While he enjoyed his work in the quarry, Cunningham worried about the dangers involved in working with steam and stone. In addition, he had a wife and a young son to think about and needed to find a "safer" profession. So the 5'11", 165-pound war veteran joined the United States Coast Guard in July 1928 as a surfman, earning about $60 per month. His first of two assignments was at the Hammond Bay station, near Ocqueoc, Michigan, on Lake Huron. There the children attended the Coast Guard School in the Presque Isle County school system and Helen kept house. The remote community was made up entirely of Coast Guard families. Cunningham continued his education, earning certificates along the way, the last one only a day before his death.

Earl Cunningham proudly served at the Hammond Bay Coast Guard Station near Ocqueoc, Michigan, on Lake Huron. Photo courtesy of the Joint Archives of Holland, Michigan.

In September 1935 Cunningham was assigned to the United States Coast Guard Station at Charlevoix, Michigan, located about 79 miles away from Hammond Bay on Lake Michigan. He arrived on September 22nd to find a house and get acquainted with his new surroundings. After learning that a Charlevoix station member was being assigned to Hammond Bay, he quickly switched houses with the man and solved the housing problem for both of them. While he described Charlevoix as "different" in a letter to Helen and the boys, he promised them they would enjoy the vast differences in community life, if only for a short time.

Saturday, February 8, 1936 began with a strong easterly wind and temperatures in the teens for fishing partners Cleo LaPeer and son Lloyd, Eugene Bearss, Claude Beardsley and his son-in-law, Clayton Brown, as they made their way onto the ice near South Point. By early afternoon the weather had turned deadly as the ice they stood on broke loose when a southerly wind came up. Soon United States Coast Guard Surfman William Woods spotted their predicament from the Charlevoix station's lookout tower and the push was on to rescue the stranded anglers.

Acting Captain George Kelderhouse assembled his men and rushed with a small skiff to South Point. Once there, Surfman Quinton Duhn started out onto the ice with the rescue craft and into the water. Soon he was able to reach the flow and secure Bearss and LaPeer and his son, leaving Beardsley and Brown behind for the next attempt. Boatswain's Mate Earl Cunningham volunteered to make his way to the remaining two men, even though he was off duty at the time. Unfortunately, blinding snowfall and rising waves forced Cunningham, Beardsley and Brown to forfeit to the wind, letting their oars rest in the boat as they awaited rescue.

This photograph, showing Helen and Earl Cunningham with sons Wayne, Richard and Hubert, was taken several years before the tragic events of February 8, 1936. The boys ranged from four to ten years old when their father died. Photo courtesy of the Joint Archives of Holland, Michigan.

While the men drifted, Captain Kelderhouse and the other members of his crew rushed back to the station to retrieve a small, 150-pound motorized dinghy. Soon they were rushing back to South Point with the new rescue craft on a horse-drawn sleigh, towing it across rough ice to open water. As they proceeded the first sled broke and another had to be located. With a new sled, they once again attempted to reach open water, but crashed through the weak ice up to their waists. Finally they reached open water and launched the small open boat and searched throughout the night, but to no avail as the missing men had steadily drifted to the north in the subzero temperatures and blinding snow.

When the searchers returned at 5:30 A.M. on Sunday, their clothing was frozen. They found that the channel was still blocked and getting worse with the northwesterly wind blowing at force 5. While Kelderhouse purchased dynamite to clear the channel and attempt a launch of the eight-ton motor lifeboat Big Bertha, the crew returned the ice-coated dinghy to the station by sleigh. Surfman Woods was taken to the hospital with frozen feet.

With the assistance of crew members and local citizens, the motor lifeboat and its crew made it to open water and spent the rest of the day looking for the lost trio, but again, they could find no sign of life. The missing men drifted farther up the lake, growing colder and less hopeful for rescue. While the local crew desperately searched for the lost trio, assistance from the Sault Sainte Marie Coast Guard Station steamed toward Charlevoix in the form of a cutter and two airplanes, one from the Detroit News and the other from the Coast Guard, but no one could find the missing men.

Around 6:00 P.M. on Sunday, Cunningham succumbed to the cold and died in Brown's arms. Conversation between Beardsley and Brown now turned to their families as they struggled to keep their blood flowing by pacing around the icebound boat. At 10:00 P.M., after moving toward the shore with Brown, Beardsley fell waist deep into the lake and was retrieved with Brown's pike pole. Soon after that Beardsley lay down on the ice and died. Knowing that he would also perish if he did not reach shore soon, Brown steadily, sometimes crawling, moved toward Good Hart, Michigan, almost nine miles away. By Monday afternoon Native Americans on the shore had sighted Brown and went to rescue the delirious and incoherent man. Authorities

A grisly scene greeted the rescuers when they found the bodies of fisherman Claude Beardsley and Boatswain's Mate Earl Cunningham on the ice of Lake Michigan on February 8, 1936. Cunningham, who volunteered to rescue the stranded fishing buddies, died of exposure in the icebound boat. Photo courtesy of the Joint Archives of Holland, Michigan.

and friends learned of his survival by telephone and rushed by ambulance to Good Hart. There they listened to his ordeal and learned of his companions' deaths.

Now the task of recovering the bodies of Cunningham and Beardsley began. After a Coast Guard chartered search plane spotted the bodies and the skiff on Tuesday, the Charlevoix crew set out to retrieve them, but poor visibility and a force 4 wind turned them back. The next day fellow Coast Guardsmen and local Native Americans returned to the ice, pulling a boat the nine miles out onto the ice. Later that day, after eight hours on the ice, they returned with the two bodies. "Two Dead, Third Survives Floe Ordeal" read the headline in the *Charlevoix Courier*, February 12, 1936, as United States Congressman John Lesinksi read "A Tribute to Heroism" in honor of Earl Cunningham on the floor of the House of Representatives in Washington, D.C.

So marked the end of an event still unmatched in the people of Charlevoix's long and tenacious relationship with Lake Michigan. Later that week, Cunningham was laid to rest at Silver Lake Cemetery in Wolverine, near Afton, and Beardsley at Charlevoix's Brookside Cemetery, while Brown lay recovering from frostbitten feet. Both men left grieving families and a shocked community that marked this as the worst ice tragedy in the history of the village.

In late March, Brown lost both of his feet to gangrene, brought on by cold and the bruises from beating them with an ax handle to keep the blood flowing. According to the newspaper, members of the U.S. Coast Guard received commendations for their "highest type of courage," a phrase that definitely described Cunningham's actions that day. A chapter about this event, entitled "Greater Love Hath No Man," was also published in a 1937 book by Karl Baarslag titled *Coast Guard to the Rescue*, and in August 1940 a plaque to all who had perished with him in the history of the United States Coast Guard was dedicated in Grand Haven, Michigan.

Postscript: After writing an article for the *Charlevoix Courier* in February 2000 about this incident, I became curious about what had happened to Helen and the three boys, then ages four, six, and ten. I knew from the newspapers that she had returned to Afton with the boys, but nothing more. After getting nowhere with the National Personnel Records Center, I turned to the internet for help in finding Cunningham's three boys, and possibly more about their father. There I discovered that all three had passed away, the last in 2000.

So I turned to Earl's grandsons. I wrote letters to men with matching first names of the boys, explaining my interest in their grandfather. After many weeks of waiting, I received a phone call from Penny Helmer of Hudsonville, Michigan, granddaughter of Earl Cunningham and daughter of Wayne, saying that her mother had received my letter and that she, Penny, wanted to visit me in Holland.

Upon her arrival she opened a box containing a family scrapbook and the medals received by Earl Cunningham during his service in the Coast Guard. It was there that I discovered that he had been nominated for a Carnegie Hero Fund Commission medal, but turned down because of his employment with the service at the time. I also discovered Coast Guardsman Cunningham's coveted Gold Life Saving Medal and other service awards, including a letter from the U.S. Treasury Department to Helen awarding her late husband the Gold Life Saving Medal "in recognition of the heroic daring displayed by him in attempting to rescue two men from drowning on February 8, 1936."

Later that week I alerted the U.S. Coast Guard Historian's Office of my find and the omission of Boatswain's Mate Earl Cunningham from the official list of medal recipients posted on their website. They quickly acknowledged the omission and have since added his name to this honored list of heroes.

Leggings, Flat Hats, and Seabags: Coast Guard Boot Camp At Cape May, New Jersey, 1951

by Frederick G. "Bud" Cooney
(Volume 6, Issue 2)

In October 1951 the Korean War was well underway and Uncle Sam was drafting young men not headed to college into national service. I had just graduated from La Salle Academy in Providence, Rhode Island, and college was not in the cards for me. I enlisted in the United States Coast Guard. I said good-bye to my folks and caught a night train to Philadelphia. There I met up with a large group of young men for the last leg of the trip to the U.S. Coast Guard Receiving Center at Cape May, New Jersey, to begin twelve weeks of boot camp. Cape May during the winter of 1951-52 was rather remote, windy, damp and cold, not quite the vacation spot we see today in the magazines.

Upon arrival we were herded onto buses to enter the new world of military obedience. Things moved very fast and strictly by the numbers once we set foot on the base. We were told to get into formation and march to designated empty barracks that would be our home for the duration of our stay. Needless to say the commands of "Fall in!" and "Forward march!" were not in our vocabulary at that time but within an hour and after some tough yelling by leaders in neat sailor uniforms, we got the hang of it.

Once gathered inside our barracks rec-deck [recreation deck] we were told that our company would be designated DOG-12, made up of three fifty-man platoons (There were no female recruits in the Coast Guard at this time). Our company commander was Chief Boatswain's Mate St. Sauveur - we pronounced it "severe" - who wore rows of wartime ribbons he earned for driving 83-foot Coast Guard rescue boats across the English

Cape May has seen this scene many, many times. Photo courtesy of Frederick "Bud" Cooney.

Channel and picking up survivors during the Normandy invasion in World War II. He also wore six impressive gold hash marks on his left sleeve indicating he had been a Coastie for at least twenty-four years. St. Severe greeted us with the kind words, "I want every one of you rotten sons-of-bitches to go to church this Sunday." How about that?

We were also told that the commanding officer of the Coast Guard Receiving Center was a World War II hero, Captain Miles H. Imaly. This stately looking officer was a veteran of the Sicily and Salerno landings and headed up the Coast Guard Landing Craft Infantry-Large (LCI-L) operations for the beach landings at Normandy on D-Day, June 6, 1944. These were our military mentors and our stay with them would not be easy. My buddy recruit's name summed it up for us. His name was Seymore Misery. No fooling.

Immediately, we were ordered to empty out our pockets and gym bags that we had been instructed to carry from home with shaving gear and change of underwear and socks. What was dumped out on the deck were cigarettes, girlie magazines, pocket knives, candy, gum, and a few condoms (at least one fellow had high hopes), and a variety of other items the "institution" considered useless while we were confined to boot camp. These items were confiscated. The gym bags with our dirty underwear were shipped back for our moms to cry over. Well, not all moms cried, I guess.

Within forty-eight hours we had donned our canvas leggings, received several large needles in both arms, had our skulls shaved clean, and been issued a full seabag that included a raincoat, two wool blankets, pillow, dress uniforms (bell-bottoms with thirteen buttons), pea coat, work clothes and two white mattress covers we called "fart sacks." These were just a few of the items that had to be stenciled, rolled or folded into neat packets and placed in precise order into forty-inch high white canvas seabags that would go around the world with us for the duration of our enlistment, blankets, pillow and all. We lived out of our seabags in boot camp. There were no lockers.

Ten, hut! Seaman "Bud" Cooney stands at attention during his early days training at Cape May. Photo courtesy of Frederick "Bud" Cooney.

The coming days and weeks would be chock-full of Coast Guard training including "Guard Week," when we learned to handle and fire the Garand .30-calibre rifle and the .45-calibre automatic pistol, taking over base security tasks. We had "Galley Week," where we took over the work of feeding hundreds of recruits and base personnel, peeling spuds, setting tables, and washing and polishing bright work. Launching and rowing a 26-foot, eight-man

Monomoy pulling boat through the winter brine was not an easy task, yet we learned to do it with perfection. This was all done under the watchful eye and instruction of permanent base personnel and designed to prepare us for a multitude of duties we would be assigned to as viable members of the oldest military seagoing service in the United States.

Looking back over the years, the twelve weeks of boot camp training provided a young man the jump-start required for Coast Guard work and skills to carry through life and maintain the Coast Guard motto, Semper Paratus.

I have returned to the town of Cape May for a few short visits over the past fifty years and have seen the changes both at the Coast Guard Receiving Center and the growth of the community, changes for the good and bad. Overall, Cape May remains a beautiful landmark on our coast.

Coast Guard Tape Resurfaces of Harrowing 1980 Rescue Off Massachusetts

by Captain W. Russell Webster, USCG (Retired)
(Volume 7, Issue 3)

Even a quarter century later, Anthony Militello, 50, skipper of the ill-fated fishing vessel *Hattie Rose*, can still feel the numbing cold of 32-degree water. "Some of the most vivid memories (of the rescue) are like snapshots in a photo album," he says.

Militello's rescuer, Bill Ross, the retired Commanding Officer of the Coast Guard cutter Cape Horn, dreams still about the night of February 7, 1980. Ross sees his rescue cutter "sliding down the backside of a huge wave in the dark," adding, "I can see (the fishing vessel) *Hattie Rose* rolling over underneath my bow. I can feel the cold and hear the screams of the men in the water."

Almost 25 years have passed since the crew of the Coast Guard Cutter Cape Horn saved six frightened fishermen from frigid North Atlantic waters off Provincetown, Massachusetts. But the fishing vessel's skipper and the cutter's captain will never forget the night that changed their lives forever. Their recollections of the rescue - both the crew of the *Hattie Rose*, and those manning the Coast Guard vessel - have been aided by a rare audiotape of distress communications that chronicles the actual terrifying events and the fear and joy that existed that stormy night.

The tape was made by Master Chief Ron Knipple, the former Officer in Charge of nearby Coast Guard Station Provincetown. Knipple directed his people to put a portable recorder near the VHF-FM marine radio speakers because he thought "a lot of people were going to die that night."

Recording equipment for Coast Guard rescue stations would not come for several years, and even then, would only be archived for just two years, making the 1980 *Hattie Rose* rescue tape all the more special. The 75-foot *Hattie Rose*, a Gloucester, Massachusetts fishing vessel with a crew of six, left the Georges Banks fishing grounds 14 hours before trouble started on February 7, 1980. The vessel was a steel hulled western rigged trawler, just three years old and in good condition. Fishing had been excellent for Militello, then 25, and his five crewmen. There was 50,000 pounds of Cod and varying species of other fish on board from just one day's effort. Normally, it would have taken six to eight days of fishing to catch this much fish.

Life on the trawler was hard work and came in repetitive cycles of effort that involved fishing, offloading, repairing, re-provisioning and refueling. However, the enticement of a typical two to three day fishing trip in 1980 would "make much better than an average week's pay from somebody working ashore," according to Militello.

But there were risks at sea that landlubbers did not have to brave. The same fish that could put bread on the table could clog the scuppers that normally allowed flooding waters go back in to the sea. If the fishing was too good, the prospect of improperly loaded fish holds could bring unforeseen instabilities that could make a boat difficult to handle, or even cause it to capsize without forewarning, even in a calm sea. And, chief among the risks for a fishing vessel was New England's unpredictable weather that could amplify any instability.

The weather was horrible the night of February 7, 1980 and continued to deteriorate as the *Hattie Rose* motored towards Gloucester. Captain Militello restlessly lay down in his bunk after dinner. Shortly thereafter, the radio crackled with the distress call MAYDAY! MAYDAY! MAYDAY! from the nearby fishing vessel *Mother & Grace*. Militello recalls "they were about seven miles to the north of us also headed for Gloucester." *Hattie Rose* quickly altered course to assist the *Mother & Grace*. Lieutenant (JG) Bill Ross from the Coast Guard cutter Cape Horn would recall just how bad the weather was that night as he and his crew got underway from safe refuge in Provincetown Harbor to respond to the distress call from the *Mother & Grace*. "The cutter's anemometer, recently calibrated in miles-per-hour, read 70 just before it blew off the yardarm." Ross remembered how the trip from

Provincetown began: "snow was blowing horizontally and so heavy that the radar was useless. Navigation was by dead-reckoning and seat-of-the-pants. Crossing 'the Race' on the way out, the tide rip was opposing the wind driven waves. The beating we took caused a number of interior furnishings to be ripped off the bulkheads."

Seas were higher than 15 feet, the contemporary safety 'ceiling' for cutters the size of the Cape Horn. Some waves that night crested above 25 feet and occasionally, 40 footers ferociously slapped the side of the hull like a giant gong. Navigation was hampered because it was impossible to put pencil to paper in the stormy conditions. Severe icing conditions added topside weight and threatened the cutter's stability, creating a hazardous ice rink for topside rescue personnel. Within a half hour of the *Mother & Grace's* problems, Captain Militello noticed his own ship felt "a bit sluggish," and he bounded from his cabin and was "shocked when he looked aft and saw that the stern was just about under water."

At about this same time, the fishing vessel *Mother & Grace* managed to resolve its troubles, and continued on its way toward Provincetown under the escort of two Good Samaritan fishing vessels. Captain Militello quickly pushed *Hattie Rose's* throttles to the firewall and ordered all pumps brought on line to help dewater the vessel. He initiated his own rescue call at 9:40 p.m. and was extremely thankful that Ross and the rescue cutter were just seven miles away because of the previous distress call.

The Cape Horn pounded her way through the maelstrom and arrived near *Hattie Rose* at 10:15 p.m. Militello's crew quickly donned their survival suits and deployed the life raft. Unfortunately, *Hattie Rose's* forward motion combined with the near hurricane force wind ripped the raft from the crew's frozen hands and carried it over the side.

At this point, Militello and his crew were spiritually crushed, seeing their raft destroyed and galloping off and capsizing in the towering waves. Now they were anxious to be lifted off the floundering vessel by helicopters from the nearby Coast Guard Air Station on Cape Cod. They had no way of knowing the crews of the HH-3 "Pelican" rescue choppers were in an 'all volunteer' status that night because of the horrendous weather. And, according to Ross, "the pucker factor was pretty big since the Coast Guard had lost an HH-3 and most of its crew eleven months earlier" in very similar circumstances trying to hoist a

47-year old crewman from a Japanese fishing vessel. Although helicopter crews would try repeatedly to get airborne this night, none would arrive until much later.

Ross knew the copters weren't coming in time but was directed to withhold this hope-draining information from *Hattie Rose's* skipper. Instead he repeatedly focused Militello on the possibility of a sea rescue that required the fishermen to voluntarily jump overboard into the frigid 32-degree water. Militello's response was predictably uncomfortable "but ah it seems awfully small to put six guys in these seas."

After inquiring when the helicopter might be arriving and being told "35 minutes," Militello knew his options were becoming limited and he became despondent, "Roger Cap, roger, oh God, God; God I don't know what to do Cap!" Ross sensed Militello's anguish and fear because Ross was afraid too, and encouraged Militello, knowing that if the ship's captain faltered, so would his crew.

"Listen Cap you just stay with her. She's uh, she's still floating...just stay with her and uh, maybe uh, you know, it will work out you get out of here and you'll be home real quick. Keep all your people together, uh gather all of the flares and lights and what ever you got uh, here and we're going to stick with you and if you go in the water we're going to pick you up as fast as we can."

The situation became even bleaker as the nearby fishing vessel Paul & Dominic asked Militello if dewatering efforts were working. Militello's voice trailed away "We can't get the pumps running. The deck... we can't clear the deck and we don't know what's flooded: our water tank, our lazarette, the fish hold - I don't know. Basically the only thing that's not flooded is the engine room - I don't know now, I still don't know. I have everybody up here so I can keep track of everybody. I can't clear the deck. I got to tell you though, we're being swamped."

Back on the Cape Horn, Ross talked with the regional rescue commander in Woods Hole about an option to fire a line over to *Hattie Rose* and pass a towing hawser. Ross lamented "but the weather conditions here are such that I don't know if they can even get anyone on deck to even catch it because their stern is under."

After an hour and half of being escorted, Militello sensed that the end was near. By this time, the Paul & Dominic had arrived on scene and began to trail the *Hattie Rose* knowing the stranded fishermen could be in the water in seconds. According to Ross "we were out of time on all fronts. To stay afloat *Hattie Rose* had been heading directly downwind and could not turn around - the engine kept running because it was well forward and the flooding was progressing from aft. Ross discussed turning around with Militello, but Militello knew that as soon as he tried the *Hattie Rose* would roll over.

At this point in the case both boats only had a couple of miles left before running into the huge breaking surf on the shoals of the backside of Cape Cod near Highland Light. Militello's situation became even more desperate "Ah, our stern is completely swamped. Jesus Christ, ah I don't want to risk it any longer, I am scared to risk it, but I don't know Cap. I don't know if we should jump over the side or not! How long is this helicopter going to take to be here?"

Ross continued to try to calm Militello, but he also began maneuvering Cape Horn closer to *Hattie Rose*, and had guardsmen stand by Cape Horn's cargo nets and get ready to throw the fishermen a line. At this point, Militello shouted to Ross, "Where'd you go, Cap!!" Ross responded, "I'm right behind you; about a ship length" The seas were so high and so close together that even though the two vessels were only 80 feet apart, when one ship crested and the other was in the trough they would periodically lose sight of each other. As the distance closed to 50 feet Militello again held out hope for an air lift rather than a water rescue "what's the word on that helicopter Cap!!"

At 11:45 p.m. the skies miraculously cleared and a Cape Cod rescue chopper finally took off, expecting to arrive between 12:05 and 12:10 a.m., but it wouldn't be soon enough and Militello and Ross both knew it. Militello indicated, "Roger Cap, I am really getting panicky here!"

Ross and Militello then discussed options for an alongside transfer of personnel direct from one boat to another, but Ross thought this was too dangerous "Ah, I just I can't put the ship alongside of her. I can't come alongside and take you off. She'll puncture the hull and we'll both go down. So I just can't do that, so uh, we're just going to have to get as close as we can, throw you lines and pick you up that way."

The distance between the two boats had closed to 35 feet. The cutter's spotlight played tricks on both crews as the men were alternately bathed in bright light and then thrust in to pitch darkness as the vessels asynchronously rolled 40, sometimes 50 degrees to either side.

Militello's voice is pleading and is occasionally drowned out by his fellow fishermen's' screams "Cap, she's all flooded, oh! If we go over the side now we're going to be lost. Twenty-five foot seas, you're never going to get us!" The skipper of the Paul & Dominic encouraged Militello to take the plunge "stay together, jot up the line and jump off together. You stay tied up to the line together. We get you, don't worry about it."

Ross had now managed to get Cape Horn to within two feet of the *Hattie Rose*, perilously close for the conditions, and a line was thrown to the beleaguered vessel and Militello's crew were finally all linked together. The time was 11:47 p.m. and Ross authoritatively told Militello "Ok, you guys got to think about doing this now!"

Militello knew the moment was near "Cap, when I say 'go,' I'm going to shut the engine down and jump with the guys. You got that Cap?" At 11:48 p.m., the Coast Guard helicopter had still not arrived in the area, but communications with helicopter CG-1484 were established with Ross. *Hattie Rose* was about to capsize and her crew were mustered and ready to jump overboard. Cape Horn was so close to *Hattie Rose* at this point that one misstep would have caused the cutter to crush Militello and his crew and possibly put a hole in the cutter.

At 11:49 p.m. Cape Horn's crew had the end of the line connected to *Hattie Rose's* crew when the fishing vessel slowly rolled over and capsized. All six fishermen jumped in to the frigid waters as Cape Horn's crew simultaneously pulled on the life line.

The cutter, now stopped, wallowed in the towering sea and slowly slid down the backside of a huge 40 foot wave. This moment is the watermark that is forever etched in Ross' memory and his night-time reminder for ages to come. Soon thereafter, the strain of bearing the weight of six fishermen snaps the life line. Four fishermen are close enough to grasp another line from the cutter and are quickly reeled in like fish to the Coast Guard vessel But all four fishermen are nearly incapacitated by the numbing cold, so two cutter crewmembers, Boatswain's Mate Third Class Duncan Grant and Seaman Thomas Jennings, bravely go over the side and help haul them aboard while Cape Horn rolled on her beam ends.

Militello and his 56-year-old Uncle Giacomo Ferrara are the last remaining crewmen to be rescued, but Ferrara is too exhausted to hang on to Cape Horn's cargo net and he lets go and slowly drifts away. Militello is faced with the choice of saving himself immediately or staying with his uncle and hoping for later rescue. He knows his uncle is too weak to keep his head up much longer, and Militello, without a lifejacket, willfully lets go of the cargo net, pushes off from the bow of the cutter and accompanies his uncle back in to the darkness towards the partially submerged *Hattie Rose*.

At this point, the helicopter had arrived in the area and Ross directed it to assist in the search for the two lost crewmen. Ross' crew quickly energized an auxiliary spotlight and with the assistance and direction of the skipper of the Paul & Dominic miraculously found Militello and his uncle in the light's pencil beam. In an effort to rescue Militello and Ferrara, Ross boldly brought his cutter about in the tumult, positioning Cape Horn within 50 feet of the overturned *Hattie Rose*. Ross' challenge at this point was to maneuver Cape Horn beam to the seas - in between the men in the water upwind - and the capsized hulk immediately downwind of him.

"Once in position, I risked killing the men with my screws, so essentially I (was in a position where I) could no longer maneuver. I dared not look at the overturned hulk at that point, and just waited for the impact...which fortunately never came, since she (the fishing vessel) slipped beneath the waves just in time."

Guardsmen Grant and Jennings again risked their own lives by going down the cargo net a second time to foist Militello and Ferrara onboard the cutter. The time was 12:20 a.m. The actual rescue took just 30 minutes. Waves of emotion flooded over the rescued and the rescuers. Ross was demonstrably elated, now talking with the helicopter "we got them all! We've got all six of them here. Unbelievable: 25-foot seas and we had them separated."

After the crews' health was verified, Ross released the helicopter to return to Air Station Cape Cod. At 3:30 a.m., February 8, 1980, Ross and Cape Horn, with Militello and his soggy crew, pulled in to Coast Guard Station Provincetown. Militello and his crew are met by family and friends who cried and sobbed uncontrollably with happiness and joy. Ross and his crew, divested of their precious human cargo, had little time to celebrate, knowing they had to return to Woods Hole to refuel and complete the rest of their assigned patrol.

Soon after this heroic rescue, the mayor and citizens of Gloucester, Massachusetts, presented Ross and his crew with a bronze medallion called "The Mariner's Medal of the City of Gloucester for Courage at Sea." Gloucester had not awarded this medal to any Coast Guard cutter before and has not awarded one since the *Hattie Rose* rescue. Bill Ross and his crew received the Coast Guard Commendation Medal along with the Coast Guard Meritorious Unit Commendation for their heroism on the night of February 7, 1980. The skipper of the *Paul & Dominic*, Gaetano Barncaleone, was awarded the Coast Guard Public Service Commendation for his heroic role in helping coordinate the rescue of Militello's crew.

Bill Ross served aboard six ships and commanded three of them in a 26 year Coast Guard career. He recently retired as a Captain and is now the Deputy Federal Security Director for the Transportation Security Administration at the Philadelphia Airport. Skipper Anthony Militello still lives in Gloucester with his wife and three children, but no longer makes his living as a fisherman.

SECTION V:
A Legacy Continues

PORTRAIT OF A DYING BREED: THE GILBERT'S BAR HOUSE OF REFUGE

by Ensign Cara Blasko, USCG

Introduction by Cindee Herrick, Curator, USCG Academy Museum (Volume 8, Issue 2)

Cara Blasko wrote this article for her Maritime History course as a first class cadet [in 2004] at the request of the Gilbert Bar House of Refuge. They had written the Academy requesting help with research. Cara found it an interesting project. They flew her to Florida to see the site and meet with their board. She also went to Washington D.C. to perform some of the research. The paper became the basis for the next layer of national level historic preservation status, thereby making it more significant than the usual student history paper. Cara is now Ensign Blasko, assigned to a Coast Guard cutter."

Background

Gilbert's Bar House of Refuge was built to shelter and protect the seamen who made it to shore following a shipwreck.During the late 1800s the Florida Coast was barren of Life-Saving Stations and thus, any mariner who washed ashore would die unless able to walk several miles to the nearest station or lighthouse. While there were not enough shipwrecks along the Florida Coast to warrant full Life-Saving Stations, it was obvious that some type of shelter was necessary. "Houses of refuge are located exclusively upon the Florida coast, where the requirements of relief are widely different from those of any other portion of the seaboard."[i] There were several undocumented shipwrecks prior to the establishment of the houses of refuge that caused [General Superintendent of the Life-Saving Service] Sumner Kimball to begin the push for another type of salvation along the coast. Houses of refuge were only built along the Atlantic coast of Florida.[1] With Kimball's urging, the Forty-third congress of June 1874 authorized the secretary of Treasury to establish "...houses of refuge for the better preservation of life and property from shipwreck..."[2] Gilbert's Bar was named as one of the five original House of refuge along the Florida coast. Sumner Kimball requested Francis Ward Chandler (1844-1926), an architect from a Boston firm, to design the houses of refuge. Chandler is credited with the design from which five houses were completed in 1876.[3]

Advertisements were then placed in newspapers all along the east coast in search of a contractor to build the houses. Albert Blaisdell of Boston replied and on October 20th, 1875, the contract and bond was signed between Blaisdell and the U.S. Treasury for five houses of refuge on the Florida coast, each to cost $2, 900 dollars.[4] The houses were almost exactly the same in design, fifteen feet wide by thirty-seven feet long with three apartments on the first floor and a second story loft. The house could accommodate twenty-five survivors with provisions for up to ten days, but there were many times at Gilbert's Bar when this number was stretched. The house for Gilbert's Bar was to be built on a piece of property on lease for twenty years from William H. Hunt. The property was just two miles north of Gilbert's Bar Inlet on a point known as St. Lucie Rocks.[5] Gilbert's Bar was completed on March 10, 1876 and is situated on "Section One of Hutchinson Island in township 38 south range 39 east."[6]

Keepers

Houses of refuge were only occupied by a keeper and his family. The keeper was not expected to row out and save shipwreck victims, but instead was required to walk the beaches following a storm in search of survivors. The average distance between houses of refuge and the nearest stations was twenty-six miles with guideposts at every mile to indicate the location of the nearest station, lighthouse, or house of refuge.[7] Frederick Whitehead was the first keeper of Gilbert's Bar House of Refuge, appointed on December 1, 1876. Whitehead received forty dollars a month for his effort and remained keeper of Gilbert's Bar until

1879.[8] During his time, Frederick Whitehead began a daily journal of the activity at the house. Ezra Stoner was the next keeper of the house and the first to receive the salary increase to $400 dollars annually. Stoner remained at the house and kept up the journal until May 26, 1880, when he was replaced by Preston A. McMillan. During the time of McMillan, a more formal "Weekly Transcript Journal" was introduced and the keeper was now responsible for keeping track of the house's cleanliness, daily weather reports, notice of passing vessels and any events that took place.[9]

McMillan was transferred to Station Indian River (FL) on Dec 16, 1881, and soon replaced by David Brown. Brown remained until March 1885 when he resigned and Thomas Peacock came from the Biscayne House of Refuge as his successor. Peacock was succeeded by Samuel F. Bunker in July of the same year. Bunker remained at the house, saving the lives of over a dozen men, until June of 1888 when he was replaced by David McClardy. McClardy resigned two years later and Hubert W. Bessey, a settler of Martin County, Florida, became keeper in 1890. Bessey stayed as keeper until 1902 when he was succeeded by Axel H. Johansen for a period of two years. Johansen was a Norwegian sea captain who was found, washed upon the shore, by a keeper's daughter near Cape Canaveral in Florida. Johansen married the keeper's daughter and served as a keeper himself at Gilbert's Bar first in 1902 and again in 1910. Johansen was transferred to Station Biscayne Bay in 1903 and William E. Rea was appointed the new keeper of Gilbert's Bar. Rea served at the house during the wrecks of the Georges Valentine and the Cosme Colzada, saving over twenty-two lives. In 1907, John H. Fromberger became the eleventh keeper of Gilbert's Bar. His tour was relatively quiet compared to Rea's and he was replaced in 1910 by the same Axel H. Johansen. Johansen remained at Gilbert's Bar during the U.S. Life-Saving Service's merge with the Revenue Cutter Service to form the modern day Coast Guard. Keeper Johansen served until 1918 when Chief Mate Charles Mason was appointed keeper. Mason served until 1930 and then was succeeded by Charles Culpepper, followed by Earl Meekins, Thomas Lewis, John Deutch, Frank Fakes, Earl Dare and Bernard Hodapp until Gilbert's Bar's decommission as a Coast Guard station in 1941.

Shipwrecks and Rescues

"Crews of surfmen are not needed here, but keepers and members of their family are required to go along the beach in both directions, in search of castaways immediately after a storm."[10] The first documented wreck was the *Bark Norina* in 1879. Over $33,000 dollars was lost when the ship sank, but the thirteen people on board were saved and brought to Gilbert's Bar for sixty-five days. In 1883, the wreck of the Schooner *Iola* reiterated the necessity of the House of Refuge when four men were rescued and brought the Gilbert's Bar. Two years later, the steamship, *America* sprang a leak causing the crew to run the vessel ashore. The ship was discovered by the keeper of Gilbert's Bar who, with his son, brought the sixteen men back to the station for shelter and food. The "Copy of Wreck Report" begins with the first entry in April 1886.

The wreck of the brig, *J. H. Lane* on the 19th of April in 1886, was the last fatal wreck of the year for the Life-Saving Service. Because only one man was employed at Gilbert's Bar, the service was not held liable for the death. The ship, with a crew of eight men and a cargo of molasses, encountered heavy weather which drove the ship so close to the shore, that the anchors were dropped in the hopes of preventing further damage. The keeper of Gilbert's Bar spotted the ship during a beach patrol about six miles south of the House of Refuge. The heavy weather remained and began to break the ship apart, so the keeper made signals to tell the men aboard the ship to come ashore. As the crew lowered a lifeboat into the surf, it was abruptly flipped over and the crew was left hanging on the lifelines. The death occurred when one man, by the name of Henry Whitlock, let go of the lifeline and was drowned. The keeper along with two other volunteers had no means of getting out to the stranded men so they watched and waited for an opportunity to save the crew. As they followed the lifeboat down the shore, an opportunity came and the keeper, with a heaving line tied around his waist, ran into the surf and grabbed hold of one of the crew members. The two volunteers remained on shore and used the heaving line to help the keeper and the crewmember back through the breaking waves. The keeper again returned to the surf until he had carried each of the seven crew members to safety. The keeper used a flask of brandy to revive the men enough to begin the eight mile journey back to

The Mosquito Lagoon House of Refuge was typical of those built along the Florida coast by the Life-Saving Service. Photo courtesy of the Osborn family.

Gilbert's Bar. Keeper Bunker exemplified the heroism and service to others that Gilbert's Bar stood for. The crew of the *J. H. Lane* left the following acknowledgment for the services they had received:

"We, the undersigned officers and crew of the brig *J.H. Lane*, which stranded on a reef six miles south of the Gilbert's Bar House of Refuge, desire to express our heartfelt thanks to Samuel F. Bunker, keeper of said station, also H.Q. Hawley and Charles Wolf, who gallantly assisted him. We would undoubtedly have perished either in the surf or on the beach but for the efforts and courage of these brave men."

In 1897, the sloop *Albatross* was rocked by a heavy squall and lost her rudder. The keeper at the time boarded the ship, anchored her to prevent further damage and brought the three people ashore. In February of 1899, a keeper was noted for his diligence when he found the vessel, *Sweetheart*, washed ashore on the beach and tried over seventeen times to re-float her. He did so successfully and the ship suffered little damage. During 1901, the keeper was forced to use his own launch to tow a ship close enough to the station for repairs. In October of 1904, there was another fatality just off the rocks of Gilbert's Bar. October 16 and 17 in 1904, the bark *Georges Valentine* from Italy was enroute from Florida to Argentina when a fierce storm blew the ship straight onto the shore, breaking her three masts. Of the twelve men on board, one was killed instantly by a falling spar and four more perished trying to reach the sand. One of the survivors headed towards the House of Refuge at Gilbert's Bar. Although the ship went aground less than one third of a mile away from the House of Refuge, the wreck could not be seen from the house due to the storm. The survivor, a man by the name of Victor Erickson, pulled another crewmember to Gilbert's Bar where they were abruptly brought in and put to bed. The keeper then set out in search for the remaining survivors. By daybreak, the keeper had brought all five of the survivors back to Gilbert's Bar and began to nurse them back to health. Had it not been for Gilbert's Bar the seven men who reached the shore would have perished soon thereafter. Below is a note of gratitude sent to General Superintendent of the Life-Saving Service in praise for the keeper's efforts:

"I, the undersigned, Prospero Mortola, captain of the Italian bark *Georges Valentine*, wrecked on the Florida coast in the vicinity of the Gilberts Bar House of Refuge on the 16th of October, about 8 p.m., would state that in that great disaster Captain Rea, the local official [keeper of the house of refuge], lent every possible aid through the night and over Sunday and Monday, succoring 7 men of a crew of 12. Thanks are due for the aid rendered during the following days up to the 29th of October, particularly to one mariner who was seriously injured, to the mate, and to the undersigned, captain, who was lacerated and bruised, and all of whom unite in expressing their gratitude to Captain Rea and the beneficial institution of the United States Life-Saving Service."[xi]

One day after the wreck of the *Georges Valentine*, the Spanish ship *Cosme Colzada* also hit the heavy storm. The quick destruction of the ship killed one man who became tangled in the rigging and forced fifteen others to swim to shore as the ship broke apart. The men made it to Gilbert's Bar where the keeper was busy with the survivors from *Georges Valentine*. Although the keeper did not see the wreck occur, he quickly began to tend to the men from the *Cosme Colzada*.[xii]

Building Integrity

The house was completed in 1876 and since then minor repairs were done in 1882 following the heavy winds of a storm. The building was fully restored in 1976 with only minor changes to the exterior including the addition of a screen to the porch and the removal of the brackets from the roof. Gilbert's Bar remains in an excellent state of integrity as the only existing Life-Saving Service house of refuge in the United States.

World War II

Following its decommission as a Coast Guard station in 1941, the United States Navy took over Gilbert's Bar just months before the attack on Pearl Harbor. Although still operated by Coast Guard personnel, Gilbert's Bar became a valuable patrol station for the Navy and was used to protect the area from U-boats and hostile aircraft during World War II. The wooden tower, which still stands today, was built by the Navy to observe German ships offshore. Coast Guardsmen worked alongside the U.S. Navy to man the watchtower and conduct patrols of the beach. Bernard Hodapp remained at Gilbert's Bar during World War II and received orders in April 1945 to completely decommission the station and lower the U. S. Flag.

Commercial Shipping

Gilbert's Bar served as an important asset to coastwise shipping during the late 1800s. The Life-Saving Service had never wanted to allow commercial and other "deep water sailors" to come ashore in their own boats following a wreck. The keepers of Gilbert's Bar had no boats of their own and thus, had no options. Keepers, such as Samuel Bunker, watched as the ship's boat capsized into the tumultuous waters tossing the crew into the sea. One of the sailors washed away and drowned, but the rest of the crew grabbed hold to the lifelines of the boat. While the boat was able to drift, landing would be impossible in the heavy surf, so Samuel Bunker tied a heaving line around his waist giving the end to two volunteers. Bunker timed the breaking of the waves and during a lull, rushed into the water, grabbed one of the sailors and dragged him to the safety of the shore. Using the heaving line, Bunker rushed into the water six more times and saved the remaining sailors from a certain death. Each of the rescued men was taken to Gilbert's Bar where they were warmed, clothed and fed.[11] This is just one example of the safety and service the Gilbert's Bar House of Refuge provided for coastwise shipping.

Present Significance

Houses of refuge were only built along Florida's Atlantic coast. Gilbert's Bar is the only surviving Life-Saving Service house of refuge and this alone qualifies Gilbert's Bar as a significant piece of architecture to the history of the United States and the United States Coast Guard. The land on which Gilbert's Bar is located has been preserved by the United States Government since 1876 for life-saving purposes. This claim to the land was challenged by Hiram E. Olds, who wanted to build a house on the land. In response, the United States Government reserved the land permanently for the purpose of Life-Saving.[xiii]

Gilbert's Bar House of Refuge was decommissioned by the government after World War II in 1945. The House was left abandoned, except for the temporary occupation by a vagrant, until 1955 when it was purchased by Martin County. The Soroptimist Club organized the Historical Society of Martin County in 1955 and campaigned to save Gilbert's Bar. Gilbert's Bar House of Refuge was declared a Historic Memorial in the State of Florida on 29 May 1969. On May 8, 1974, Gilbert's Bar was listed on the National Register for the Preservation of Historic Places, entitling it to funds for restoration. By 1976, Gilbert's Bar House of Refuge was fully restored. Today Gilbert's Bar House of Refuge serves as a maritime museum in Stuart, Florida. Turtle and lobster research is also carried out on the site.

National Significance

From Sumner Kimball, Life-Saving Service Annual Report of 1878, "The first of these embraces the eastern coast of Florida and contains only houses of refuge, which contemplate no other life-saving operation than affording succor to shipwrecked persons who may be cast ashore, and who, in the absence of such means of relief, would be liable to perish from hunger and thirst in the desolate region." Houses of Refuge played an important role in the lives of those who wrecked upon the desolate shores of Florida. For over fifty people, Gilbert's Bar House of Refuge saved their lives. The House of Refuge is the only remaining testament to the values of Honor, Respect and Devotion to Duty that the keepers exemplified and are the core values in today's Coast Guard.

Gilbert's Bar is not only nationally important because of the action of the Life-Saving Service, but also because of the House's service during World War II and the protections it afforded to commercial shipping in the twentieth century.

Protecting The Emerald Isle: The Royal National Lifeboat Institution In Ireland

by Nicholas Leach
(Volume 8, Issue 1)

The Royal National Lifeboat Institution is essentially a British organisation but unusually its operations encompass not only the British Isles but also Ireland. When the Institution was founded in 1824, Ireland was part of the British Empire and so the RNLI provided the country's lifeboats. The Institution's role during the nineteenth century was the same as in other parts of the United Kingdom, and the Irish stations were operated along lines identical to elsewhere. However, when the Irish Free State was formed and the country was divided, this role was called into question. The Treaty establishing an Irish Free State was signed on 6 December 1921, ratified by the Irish Government on 7 January 1922 and, although the six northern counties remained part of the United Kingdom, the RNLI found itself operating lifeboats in a country no longer under the rule of the British government.

Following such major changes to the political landscape, the question arose of the continuance or otherwise of the Institution's activities in Ireland. The Coastguard, run by the British Government, withdrew from the Irish Free State so should the RNLI follow suit? The Institution's independent and voluntary status, together with the value of its work, undoubtedly had a major bearing on the favourable attitude of the Irish government towards it at a time when other British organisations were too much a part of the old regime to consider retaining and the matter was quickly resolved. After correspondence between the Irish Free State Provisional Government and the RNLI, a deputation from the RNLI's Committee of Management met the Minister for Home Affairs in Dublin

The 35-foot, 6-inch Liverpool motor lifeboat Herbert John *being launched over skids laid across the beach at Youghal, County Cork, on 4 August 1952. She was on station at Youghal from 1952 to 1966. Photo supplied by Brendan O'Driscoll.*

in October 1922 to seek the new Government's opinion as to the continued role of the Institution in the new country. The Provisional Government were very positive about the Institution's work, requesting that it continue to function as it always had done and maintain the Republic's lifeboat service.

Following the Government's request to continue to be responsible for sea rescue, the RNLI reported in its Annual Report for 1925 that 'a proof of its [the Irish Free State's] desire to help … has been given by the Governor-General, who has accepted the invitation to become Patron of the Irish Free State District of the Instituition.' Soon afterwards, the Governor of Northern Ireland, the Duke of Abercorn, became Patron of the Northern Ireland District, and these new Patrons both quickly issued public appeals in the country on behalf of the RNLI with the hope that 'the Irish people will … contribute to the funds of the Institution sufficient to pay for the maintenance of the Irish Stations'. At the same time, the Irish Ministry of Industry and Commerce promised it would 'extend to the work [of sea rescue] every faculty in its power' and this arrangement has endured up to the present day.

While the issue of organising the service was being debated, funding Ireland's lifeboat stations in the 1920s remained of major concern. The priority of the newly-formed Irish Government during the decade was to repair the damage inflicted on the economy by the Troubles of 1916-23, improve housing and social conditions for the people, and this unsurprisingly took precedence over allocating funds for rescue services. However, with the RNLI maintaining its commitment to provide a lifeboat service on both sides of the Irish Sea, rescue services were hardly affected and operations continued almost seamlessly.

In 1924, two years after the creation of the Irish Free State, the RNLI celebrated its Centenary. In Ireland, the celebrations were undertaken with as much enthusiasm for the Institution's work as elsewhere. Yet it was the finances and voluntary spirit that featured most prominently in the Centenary speeches in Ireland. At a meeting of the Dublin Branch, the Chairman, the Right Hon Andrew Jameson, urged those present to make every effort to increase the Institution's income in Ireland. A leading article in the *Irish Times* at the time stated 'It is a national need of first importance that their efficiency shall not be impaired through lack of funds.' The Belfast Newsletter stated: 'The

Relief lifeboat Lord Saltoun *launches down the slipway at Baltimore in southwest Ireland. Photo by Nicholas Leach.*

peculiar glory of the Service is that it is voluntary, and therein lies not only the secret of the splendid efficiency of the rescue work, but the high interest and the long-continued support which the people as a whole have given to the organisation [sic].'

Appeals were launched during the centenary year by many fundraising branches in Ireland, as the economics of Ireland's lifeboat service continued to be uppermost in the minds of those involved in its operation. In 1931, when new lifeboats were named and dedicated at Courtmacsherry Harbour, Ballycotton and Youghal, President Cosgrave, in attendance at all three ceremonies, appealed to the people of the Free State to come forward generously in support of 'this great humane and heroic service.' He also made it clear that the work of the Institution in the newly-founded country was highly valued: 'On behalf of the people of this country I wish to pay a warm tribute to the splendid work done by the Lifeboat Institution… I am glad to feel that the support given to the Institution in Ireland is increasing and I feel sure it will continue to grow as the people become better able to appreciate the service.' Such sentiments have continued to be expressed ever since.

Despite the positive attitude of the authorities in the Irish Republic, the position of the RNLI in Ireland remains something of an anomaly. Although proposals for the formation of an Irish Executive never came to fruition, in 1970 Irish members of the Committee of Management started informal meetings with senior RNLI staff in Ireland which resulted in improved knowledge for both parties. In the same year an annual subvention to the RNLI of £10,000 was inaugurated, which soon rose to £20,000 and is now £100,000. No strings are attached to this grant, obviating fears that it might impair the ability of a charitable institution to raise voluntary subscriptions. This fear has been dispelled in Ireland, and during the 1980s appeals in Dublin and Belfast were so successful that they provided new all-weather lifeboats for Howth and Donaghadee respectively. The RNLI also receives support with infrastructure development such as berths, dredging and so on.

In 1989, a new 52ft Arun lifeboat intended to serve as a relief lifeboat specifically in the Irish Division, named Hibernia (ON.1150) during a formal ceremony at Howth, was funded from monies provided for in the Irish Sailors and Soldiers Land Trust Act 1988, the trustees of which were the Irish Government. While this is one of the more visible results

Castetownbere's lifeboat crew on board 52-foot Arun lifeboat Roy and Barbara Harding. *Castletownbere is one of the newest lifeboat stations in Ireland and this lifeboat served there for six years until she was replaced in 2004 by a brand new craft purpose-built for the station.* Photo by Nicholas Leach.

of donations, fund-raising for 'The Lifeboats', as the service is known in Ireland, continues with as much vigour as anywhere else in the British Isles and the Irish Government is more than happy for the RNLI to continue to organise the lifeboat service in Ireland. The cost of maintaining a rescue service is considerable and the majority of money spent in Ireland comes, in fact, from the United Kingdom. In 2003, for example, EUR2.2 million was raised by fund-raising in Ireland, as against the EUR13 million needed to run the lifeboat service excluding capital expenditure. However, as lifeboats benefit all users of British and Irish coastal waters, the RNLI believes that it should make up any shortfall between funds raised in the Republic and the amount actually needed to equip and run the country's lifeboats.

Testament to this is the increase in the number of lifeboat stations in the country, particularly on the west coast, during the 1990s providing

The 17-meter Severn class lifeboat Katie Hannan *leaves her station on exercise. Portrush is one of the stations that covers the north coast of Ireland. Photo by Nicholas Leach.*

proof of the RNLI's continued commitment to its role in Ireland. Today, in 2005, forty-three RNLI lifeboat stations are located strategically around the coastline of Ireland (including two new stations based on the large Lough Derg, Lough Erne Upper and Lough Erne Lower) as well as the additional inshore rescue boats operated by either the Irish Coast Guard or the Community Inshore Rescue Service as 'declared resources' for Search and Rescue (SAR).

Ireland's lifeboat stations are an integral part of the RNLI's service, and the country is treated no differently than the other part of the UK in which the RNLI maintains lifeboats. Operationally, the country is one unit - the Inspectors for Ireland cover every station in both north and south - and the stations operate with the same personnel and structure as those in England, Scotland or Wales. The country is divided into two regional fund-raising areas with offices at Belfast and Dun Laoghaire to reflect the political administrations. Throughout Ireland the RNLI is seen as an organisation from which all can benefit - it is 'the lifeboat service' for shared coastal waters, and as a humane organisation can rise above political and religious differences.

A Day In The Life of Coast Guard Station Point Allerton

by John J. Galluzzo
(Volume 6, Issue 4)

Machinery Technician Second Class (MK2) Sean Hagerty's day started in the middle of the night. At 0100 on Saturday, June 14, a boater lost in the fog off Long Island, Boston Harbor, radioed the Coast Guard for help. As Officer of the Day (OOD) for his duty section, Hagerty's responsibilities included rousting a boat crew from a dead sleep and getting them on their way to finding and aiding the missing boater.

"The guy had no idea how to navigate," said Hagerty. "He said, 'Bring me out to Deer Island and I'll find my way back to Lynn.' The guys brought him to Deer Island, and he started heading right back to Boston." The Coast Guard crew then called back to the station that they would be taking the boater and his 25-foot *Wellcraft* all the way back to Lynn. They returned to the station just inside Pemberton Point at 4 a.m.

Machinery Technician Third Class (MK3) Chris Spaeth is standing watch in the communications (comm) center at 1100 as Seaman (SN) Greg Haskins, a Worcester, Massachusetts, native, sits alongside and observes, part of the nonstop training a Coast Guardsman undergoes while in uniform. Spaeth, who arrived at Point Allerton from a tour on the 210-foot cutter *Decisive*, homeported in Mississippi, is keeping tabs on one of the station's two 41-foot utility boats, this morning providing security for the turnaround of the USS Constitution in Boston Harbor.

The foul weather that has prevailed over New England for most of the spring has kept boaters off the water for the most part. Last year by this time the crew at Point Allerton had responded to 149 recorded search and rescue cases (many minor incidents go unrecorded) on their way to a yearly total of 349, the Coast Guard's fiscal year (running from October 1 to September 30). The early morning rescue brought this year's total up to 125, well off the 2002 pace.

Even the month of June has been slow. In June of 2002 the crew tended to 20 rescue cases in the first thirteen days; this year, they've been called to 12.

"It's started to pick up over the past few weeks," says Spaeth. "But it hasn't been that extreme. It's good for us, as nobody's been in danger of dying out there, but it can get pretty boring."

Even though the season began slowly, personnel movements have left Point Allerton shorthanded, creating added workload for those men and women still around. The annual spring opening of Station - Scituate, a substation of Point Allerton, the fourth largest small boat station in the Coast Guard, pulled six crewmembers away from the parent station. The upgrading of Station - Boston, formerly a station-small under Point Allerton and now a stand-alone command, drew a number of bodies away as well. A standard duty section a month ago consisted of 22 people. Today it holds just 13.

"And we've lost eight people just to transfers," says Hagerty. While aiding in family and schooling issues, the Coast Guard's policy of early summer transfers leads to problems for stations gearing up for heavy summer workloads. At a time when experienced boat drivers are needed most, many stations find themselves breaking in coxswains who are ignorant of the whereabouts of many of the area's most dangerous underwater rocks and shoals.

This morning the comm center has been unusually quiet for a Saturday. An early morning fog obscured the view of even the windmill outside the station's windows. A search for a missing kayaker off the southern end of Nantasket Beach kept the VHF radio speakers rimming the room chattering all day on Friday, as the Coast Guard sent both boats and helicopters out to find him or her. "That was a $50,000 effort that turned up nothing," says Hagerty. "Two helos, $4500 an hour to operate them for seven hours, it adds up." The kayak, when spotted, did have a lifejacket inside, not a good sign as far as the Coast Guard is concerned.

Today, Hagerty is testing out a new piece of equipment, a handheld internet-based personal information access law enforcement device that he can use to retrieve information on any registered vehicle, a person's criminal background, or anything else that simply has a serial number. In the case of the missing kayaker, for instance, the device could be used to track the sale of the watercraft back to a store, and possibly a buyer. "That could take time, but it could still be of great help," says Hagerty.

The 3.5-inch, 4-ounce CyberFORCE handheld has been tested in Florida, and Group - Boston, and Station - Point Allerton is its second stop. For the moment, Hagerty is the only one to carry the device at the station, and all questions for CyberFORCE will go through him. In time, a device will go out with each coxswain underway on the water.

The device also features automatic logoff protection. "That way nobody can pick it up on the street and use it if we lose it."

Hagerty reads the day's weather forecast, posted on sliding information boards for viewing from the watchstander's position, calling for rain and fog to move in later in the day. The information is posted alongside the day's tide chart, sunrise and sunset times, nautical charts, and other pertinent information.

"We've got 6-month recerts [re-certifications] to deal with," Hagerty explains. "We have to run dewatering drills, fire drills, keep our quals [qualifications] up. Our deadline is Monday. A STAN [Coast Guard standardization] team will be here from Ilwaco, Washington, to put the coxswains, engineers, and boat crews through tests, written and underway, and to run inspections." Asked if the small caseload has allowed some freedom to catch up on such requirements, Hagerty says, "We have no down time. Search and rescue cases are down, but law enforcement cases are up."

At 1135, the phone rings, and the VHF speakers start squawking. Ten minutes later, Coast Guard Auxiliarist Connie Reynolds arrives to relieve Spaeth as watchstander. Reynolds, a full time nurse, is volunteering 8 hours today to field calls and spell some of the active duty personnel. Attached to Flotilla 12-8 in Scituate, Reynolds spends time underway with the Auxiliary in the flotilla's area of responsibility (AOR), the North River, South River and Marshfield's Green Harbor. Today she'll oversee Point Allerton's entire AOR, from 42 degrees, 28 minutes north latitude in the north (Little's Point, Swampscott) to 42 degrees, 5 minutes north latitude in the south (Green Harbor).

Officer of the Day Sean Hagerty shares the comm. Center console of Station Point Allerton with Auxiliarist Connie Reynolds on Saturday, June 14, 2003. Although the day started off slowly, it soon became the busiest in months. Photo by John Galluzzo.

"There's been no weather, no small craft warnings, no SARs [search and rescue cases], nothing," says Spaeth. "Not a typical day. Not much going on."

Reynolds, who grew up in nearby Weymouth, says she enjoys the job of watchstander. "You have to know every buoy, every inlet of the AOR. You answer to the OOD. And my boss always reminds me that when you're doing this job, you have to remember that you're the voice of the Coast Guard.

"It can be very interesting. It's the big picture. I know almost everything that's going on, who's out there, what they're doing. You get to know the active crew pretty well."

At 1159, Reynolds fields her first call, from Coast Guard Auxiliary boat 201777. They transfer coordinates of a telephone pole floating in the water, 15 feet long by 1 foot in diameter, off Scituate's Minot Beach. Hagerty tells Reynolds to call Group - Boston, who will broadcast a notice to mariners over the VHF. She also calls the Scituate Harbormaster.

At 1203, Hagerty calls Boatswain's Mate Second Class (BM2) Steve Pickard, Fireman (FN) Carlton Pettigrew, and Seaman (SN) Jeremiah Loser (pronounced Lo-zher) and SN Matt Friedler to the comm center to prepare to get underway. Within minutes all four appear, and Hagerty unlocks the strong box holding the station's handguns. Each is handed a 9-millimeter Beretta and several clips. Donning their gear, including bulletproof vests and bright orange "float coats," they head out the backdoor of the station toward the boathouse and *CG 41354*, a 41-foot utility boat. Clearing their weapons before they board the boat, they're ready for a routine patrol of the area.

Four kayakers are inside Pemberton Point, as is the red tugboat *McDevitt Girls*. Heading west around Peddock's Island, coxswain Pickard calls out "Comin' up!" to warn his crew that the boat's speed is about to increase. Pettigrew, Loser and Friedler act as spotters for Pickard watching not only for other boats, but obstructions that may be in the water.

Off the north end of Peddock's, a garbled transmission comes over the radio. Pickard drops the power to the engine to listen for orders. Instead, he hears, "Child playing on the radio, you need to get off VHF 16 right now. Coast Guard out." Hoping for something to break the season's boredom, Pickard says, "It's been a crappy summer so far. It seems if you aren't out doing it for training, you aren't out doing it at all."

41354 continues around Peddock's and heads back to the station. Forty minutes underway, and nothing to report. The crew ties up the boat in the south side of the boathouse, refuels, and heads back to the building, again clearing their weapons before heading inside.

In the comm center, a buzz is in the air. 2003 cases 126, 127 and 128 are about to happen simultaneously, and all are taking place around Scituate, to the south. A boat has run aground in the North River, and at 1259 a call comes in from a boat aground in the South River. The Marshfield Harbormaster responds to the South River call, as BM3 Jeremiah Lukkes, SN Kyle Pavao and SN Brain Morrarty head from the North River to the South River in their 21-foot rigid hull inflatable boat (RHIB), having helped the first boat get clear.

"Coast Guard, we are in a thirty-foot boat with a red hull, but we don't know exactly where we are," says the voice from the South River.

The Marshfield Harbormaster, though, is within view of the disabled boat. "I can see you. I'll be there in a few seconds." TowboatUS, a private salvage company, has heard the conversation and is on the way as well. By the time that the Coast Guard arrives, at 1307, the sailboat is being pulled off.

Hagerty looks to Pickard. "I think we're gonna have a busy day. We're gonna be real busy when the fog rolls in." He then picks up the VHF mike. "Coast Guard 210601, Station Point Allerton. Check out that boat and make sure it's seaworthy. Over."

At 1315, a third call comes in. "Coast Guard, this is the ______. I've had a fire on board, I've put it out. My Loran is not up. My position is 42 degrees, 7 minutes, 8 seconds north latitude, 70 degrees, 39 minutes west longitude. I will require assistance towing."

"He's off Humarock," says Reynolds.

"Coast Guard 210601, Station Point Allerton. Boat fire, off Humarock Beach, one person on board. What is your position?" calls Hagerty.

"Point, 601. We are three nautical miles away," answers Lukkes.

Hagerty grabs a wheel to determine an estimated time of arrival for their boat to the scene of the boat fire, measuring speed and distance.

"Vessel in distress, Coast Guard Station Point Allerton. Our boat is en route and will be there in eight minutes."

"I'm doing OK," comes the response.

"Can you tell us the source of the fire?"

"Smoke was coming out of the engine. I have two fire extinguishers and a halon system." At 1328, the station loses radio contact with their own boat. Hagerty looks out the window and sees the sun breaking through, contrary to the weather reports.

"They're all gonna see the sun and say, 'Hey, we can get in three hours of fishing.' Then that fog is going to come in, and the tide is going to go out," he says to Reynolds.

At 1333, BM3 Lukkes calls in over a crackling radio. "There's some smoke coming from the vessel, but it could have just been an exhaust leak. We're not sure at this time. TowboatUS is alongside. They're headed for Green Harbor."

"601, Point. RTB. [Return to Base]. Moor up and prepare for patchy fog and rain later."

Reynolds has three case folders out at her workspace. SN Haskins is helping her fill out the information necessary to document the day's events. When specifics are missing, they call around to the Scituate crew and TowboatUS for details. Hagerty, who has already been awake and on duty for more than twelve hours, shakes his head and calls Chief Warrant Officer Patrick Higgins, commanding officer of the station. "Just an update, Cap'n. We've just run three cases in a half hour. I don't know how anybody can run aground at high tide, but we've had two groundings." With four cases in one day, June 14, 2003, is the busiest day the station has seen since October 5, 2002.

At 1408, the VHF speakers are bursting with information. Calls are coming into the Coast Guard stations at Merrimac River, Gloucester, and Portsmouth, New Hampshire to the north, and Woods Hole to the south. At 1410, BM3 Lukkes calls forward to state that the Scituate boat has moored and they are headed into the station. Any further communications will have to be by landline for the time being. At 1411, Coast Guard Group - Boston relays a hazard to navigation broadcast regarding the telephone pole in the water off Scituate.

At 1412, BM2 Pickard rushes up the stairs from the rec deck [recreation room]. "Have you guys heard what's going on in Tillamook? There's a search going on for people in the water. Fox News Channel has some amazing footage of the 47-footer going over the bar." The charter fishing vessel *Tiki Tooo* has been struck by a wave, tossing nineteen people into the water off Barview, Oregon. Coast Guard Station - Tillamook has responded, as has the air station at Hammond to the north, sending helicopters and rescue swimmers to the scene. Several people are confirmed dead, several have been rescued, and two are missing.

Ten minutes later, Chief Warrant Officer Higgins stops into the station, on his day off. He carries a Nextel mobile phone with him at all times, so as to be available when his crew needs him. His wife and daughter are off in Montana setting up what will be their new home when Higgins retires from the Coast Guard this August, and Higgins is finishing up needed chores around the house. Sitting in his office, he calls a young Coastie over.

"Hey Chad," he says to BM3 Chad Fitzpatrick. "When are you due to qualify as a coxswain?"

"Mid-July, Cap'n."

"Well, I might throw a wrench into your plans. I need someone for a coxswain ceremony as part of my retirement. Is it OK with you if we push you back a little bit?"

"Sure, Cap'n, I can slack off for a month," Fitzpatrick says with a smile. Higgins looks across the hall and sees Hagerty seated at his desk, pen in hand, head thrown back in an impromptu, unexpected nap. A thorough professional, his only fault today is being human. A call over the intercom wakes him, and Higgins laughs at his OOD as he snaps forward.

"Long day, Sean?"

"Sure is, Cap'n," says Hagerty, shaking the cobwebs.

At 1510, Higgins takes a call from Hagerty on the Nextel. A tanker has called asking for help. A man on a small boat with a high-powered camera has been taking close-up pictures of the propeller, pilothouse, and other points of interest. When approached by the Coast Guard he becomes animated, shouting that he's a lawyer and that his brother is a former governor of a neighboring state. After a few minutes, he calms down and begins to comply with the Coast Guard. In a post-9/11 world, his actions throw up red flags all around.

At 1605, fog has started to creep in. Word from Tillamook is that nine are now dead, eight saved, two still missing. Ten minutes later the station's 21-footer is headed into Dorchester Bay on patrol. By 1645 the fog has again retreated. At 1650, the cook has called for the piping of the evening meal. With such a small crew on hand, he has had the liberty of asking each individual how he or she would like his or her steak cooked. Auxiliarist Reynolds opts to eat in the comm center. "That's the boys' time in the mess deck, and I don't want to interfere." She's been invited to join them, but she prefers to let them have whatever conversations young men have without her being a distraction. The mess deck has traditionally been a center of camaraderie in the Coast Guard, from its earliest days. Things have not changed. The crew makes fun of the cook, who takes it all good-naturedly. They trade other wild stories for the brief few moments they have together in relaxation.

At 1745, the returning boat crew sits down to eat with Hagerty and BM2 Steve Allen. At 1825, dead silence fills the comm center. The sun is out, the temperature is dropping, but for the moment the world of Coast Guard Station - Point Allerton is at peace. At 1835, Group Boston sends out its nightly Notice to Mariners.

Seaman Benjamin Loser, right, and Boatswain's Mate Second Class Steve Pickard clear their weapons upon returning from a routine patrol of Boston Harbor aboard a 41-foot utility boat on Saturday, June 14, 2003. Photo by *John Galluzzo.*

Forty minutes later, Station - Scituate calls in that their boat is tied up, but out of commission, stuck in reverse. Hagerty, a machinery technician, tries to talk BM3 Lukkes through a repair, meanwhile making plans to swap boats. He sends every available set of hands to the parking lot below to test a trailered boat, and prepares it to splash in Scituate. He jokes with Lukkes over the phone. "Jerry what are you doing to me? Three boats in four days. Make some arrangements with the Harbormaster to get the boat pulled from the water. And Jerry? Make sure there's no cameras around." The last line is in reference to a recently retired Scituate Harbormaster who delighted in showing off a picture of his boat towing a disabled Coast Guard boat into Scituate Harbor.

At 2000, SN Jeremiah Loser relieves Connie Reynolds as watchstander. At 2007, Lukkes calls from Scituate that the boat has been repaired, and Hagerty calls off any swap, relieved that he won't be up all night working on it, still awake after nineteen hours straight on duty. At 2023, sunset, the American flag is lowered.

BM2 Pickard, though, needs a little more time underway at night to meet his recerts for Monday, and informs Hagerty he'll be taking a crew out after dark. MK3 Spaeth, who started the day as a watchstander, FN Pettigrew and FN Kenny Wigfall all head for CG 41492. At 2050, BM2 Allen and a crew get underway on a 21-footer. Both boats are less than five hundred yards from the station when they throw on their flashing lights and stop separate boats.

Pickard stops a small fishing boat passing out of Hull Gut with four men aboard, one of whom is obviously drunk. He calls Hagerty, who runs his driver's license info through CyberFORCE, coming up with a negative response. Pickard checks the boat for lifejackets, and sends them on their way. "I can't wait to get one of those things on the boat," he says, referring to the handheld Internet device. "It'll make things so much easier." As he speaks, fireworks blast in the skies over Quincy at 2058. It's Flag Day.

At 2125, the crew of 41492 is just off Logan Airport. Pickard stops another vessel. "Guess who gets to be the next to have his name run through the machine," he quips. A family of five is on a powerboat heading out of the harbor. All three children come out of the pilothouse wearing lifejackets. As all looks to be in order, Pickard lets them go.

Stopping the boat in the middle of the harbor, Pickard, a native of Lake Placid, New York, steps out into the open air. He talks of how he's done everything he's wanted to in the Coast Guard, and is weighing his options for the future. He'd like to stick with law enforcement, either with the Customs Service or a state police outfit. But he may ultimately decide to continue with his current service.

The full moon is now perfectly visible in the east. After a quick run alongside the Boston World Trade Center building, 41492 heads for the outer harbor. At 2200 sharp, a state police boat flashes its lights to get the Coast Guard's attention and pulls alongside. MK3 Spaeth joins Pickard on deck.

The cop, alone on the small boat, tells of how he was responding to a death threat on the lives of the Park Rangers on George's Island when he stumbled across something unexpected. "They weren't there anyway. They went home for the night, so there was no danger, but I figured I should check it out. So I went to the island and found a boat I thought looked suspicious. I shined the light on it and all of a sudden all these topless women and naked men jumped up and started running around."

"Oh, man," says one of the Coasties in the darkness. "We picked the wrong boats to stop."

The cop then explains that he's headed up the Charles River, as a Wilsons concert, featuring the surviving members of the Beach Boys, is just getting out. Pickard radios BM2 Allen, who agrees to run alongside the cop and help keep watch over the flow of boats leaving the river.

At 2213, 41492 pulls back into the boathouse at Point Allerton. By 2220, all is quiet once again in the comm center. SN Loser is still working with SN Haskins, who has been on duty since 0730, quizzing him on his chartreading skills. Loser himself is preparing for a chance to go to rescue swimmer's school. BM2 Pickard is locking the handguns away. Somewhere in the station, MK2 Hagerty is finally sound asleep.

But the day never ends for the United States Coast Guard. At any minute that VHF could bark, and every available body will somehow react to the call.

"A Day in the Life of Coast Guard Station Point Allerton" originally appeared in the June 19, 2003 edition of the *Hull Times*, as part of the author's series, "A Day in the Life of Hull, Massachusetts."

The Life-Savers of Coast Guard Station Tillamook Bay, Oregon

by Dennis L. Noble
(Volume 7, Issue 1)

A major problem in writing about the U.S. Life-Saving Service and the U.S. Coast Guard centers on the lack of information concerning the people at the stations. Most writers are more interested in wrecks and rescues performed by the lifesavers than the lifesavers themselves. Very few people in the United States know anything about the people who served in the U.S. Life-Saving Service. Unfortunately, fewer still know about those serving in the modern-day U.S. Coast Guard stations along the West Coast of the United States, or anywhere else. A few U.S. Coast Guardsmen have broken this generality. Retired Master Chief Boatswain's Mate Thomas McAdams, of the Yaquina Bay, Oregon, Station is one, as is retired Chief Warrant Officer F. Scott Clendenin, also of the Yaquina Bay Station. While working on another project, I decided to focus attention on the people of a station in Oregon. As any veteran will quickly tell you, one of the first things one learns in the military is never to volunteer for anything. Some of the crew of U.S. Coast Guard Station Tillamook Bay, Oregon, however, were willing to ignore this aphorism and respond to questions about themselves and their station.

The station, located in Garibaldi, Oregon, lies approximately fifty-five miles south of the dangerous Columbia River and is in a rural area. The last population figure given for the town was 899. Ten miles to the south of Garibaldi is Tillamook, with a population of 4,400, and fifty-five miles to the north is Astoria, with a population of 9,813. A young woman from Queens, New York, just assigned to Tillamook Bay, almost tearfully said, "My backyard is bigger than this town."[1] The weather also does not cooperate. Winters, although mild, bring strong winds and a large amount of rain. Summers are cool, with less rain. A sweltering day in summer is 80-degrees Fahrenheit. This is a good station for those who like to hunt, fish and hike. On a clear day - and there are such days despite indications to the contrary - the hills forested with Douglas Fir overlooking the station can inspire one to attempt oil painting.

Three station buildings define three periods of Coast Guard history at Tillamook Bay. Photo by John Galluzzo.

There has been a boat station in the Tillamook Bay area since 1907, then a U.S. Life-Saving Service unit and located in the town of Barview, approximately two miles north of Garibaldi. The U.S. Coast Guard built a new lifeboat station in 1946 in Garibaldi.[2] An even newer station building, docks and boathouse were built in 1981 (with the barracks completed the following year) and commissioned in 1986, located closer to the bay.[3] The old lifeboat station's location placed it across busy Highway 101, the main north-south coastal highway along most of the west coast. The crew had to run across this highway to their boats. Anyone who has seen the Oregon coastal tourist traffic in the summer on Highway 101 will marvel that anyone could safely make the dash. Today, the older station buildings, called the "upper station" by the crew, contain quarters for the Officer-in-Charge, the Executive Petty Officer (XPO), Engineering Petty Officer (EPO), and barracks and dining area for the crew. Because the newer station is small, the ready boat crew remains at the newer station, while the second boat crew is at the upper station. The newer station also has a haul out facility to work on the unit's boats, shops and offices. When the search and rescue alarm rings, the ready boat crew runs down a long dock to their boat and one former Executive Petty Officer quipped that he thought there should be oxygen bottles placed at strategic intervals along the dock.

At the time of this study (2003) Master Chief Boatswain's Mate Lars Kent was the Officer-in-Charge of Station Tillamook Bay. Master Chief Kent was born in 1958. At one time, his father's profession took the family to Lima, Peru, and as a result Lars speaks fluent Spanish. When he entered the U.S. Coast Guard, on 19 January 1979, at the age of twenty, Lars listed his hometown as Coeur D'Alene, Idaho. Master Chief Kent said that he decided to enter the Coast Guard because he had quit college and "before I approached my dad I figured he might not kill me if I had an alternative plan in hand."

Master Chief Kent has served twice at Station Seattle, Washington, the cutter *Mellon*, in Seattle, Station Neah Bay, Washington, Station Coos Bay, Oregon, Station Tillamook Bay (1990-1994), the cutter *Storis*, at Kodiak, Alaska, as XPO of Station Cape Disappointment, as Officer-in-Charge of the patrol boat *Barracuda* and began serving as Officer-in-Charge of Tillamook Bay in July 2002.

Master Chief Kent has been married to Tonya for seventeen years. They have two children and one granddaughter.

Master Chief Kent said a unique feature of their area of operations is that they have three breaking bars: at Netarts, to the south of the unit, Tillamook Bay and Nehalem Bay, to the north of the station. The most dangerous aspect of the unit's area of operations is that Nehelem and Netarts are extremely shallow, while Tillamook "has several shoals directly off the west entrance that can generate large breaks [breaking waves] under the right circumstances." Furthermore, Tillamook Bay has "five rivers emptying into the bay. Periods of heavy rain, or large tide changes, can generate an outgoing current that runs in excess of 7-knots. That strong a current meeting with large incoming seas can generate a very rough bar."[4]

When questioned what he most enjoyed about being Officer-in-Charge at Tillamook Bay, Master Chief Kent responded that he felt it was the "opportunity to mentor the up and coming leadership of the Coast Guard." He said that he enjoys "working the motor lifeboat in the surf and... to show break-in surfmen how to drive in that extreme environment." On the other hand, like many Officers-in-Charge, Master Chief Kent says the downside of being an Officer-in-Charge is that he no longer spends much time actually working cases. "Now my life revolves around paperwork and personnel issues. But on occasion I still get to run a case, or get out to do training."

Master Chief Kent estimates that he has personally saved twelve people from danger. He recalls what happened in a two-day period when he was a Boatswain's Mate First Class (BM1) on his first tour at Tillamook Bay. On 14 December 1992, the 80-foot fishing vessel *Kodiak* capsized on the Tillamook Bay bar. The coxswain of the 44-foot motor lifeboat, CG 44409, operating in 14- to 16-foot breaking waves, cracked his ribs and bruised his leg. The coxswain had to remain offshore the entire night, battling seas up to 20-feet in height. The next morning, a helicopter from U.S. Coast Guard Air Station Astoria, picked up BM1 Kent and, in seas that remained at 14- to 16-feet in height, he was lowered aboard the 44-foot motor lifeboat. The official report of the maneuver said, "The hoist was described as very scary, difficult and rough." Kent then briefed the tired crew and took the motor lifeboat safely across the bar.

Two days later, on 16 December, BM1 Kent was at home when he received a call to immediately return to the station. Arriving at the unit, he learned that the ready motor lifeboat and back up boat had departed on a flare sighting on the Tillamook Bay bar and the ready motor lifeboat and back up boat were on scene. Shortly thereafter, the communications watchstander received a report that one of the motor lifeboats had rolled. Kent went to the lookout tower. From there, via the radio, he determined that the rolled boat's coxswain was not injured, and the coxswain of the back up boat was having difficulty in the high seas and wind. Twice the coxswain said over the radio that he was "at the end of his rope." Without hesitation, BM1 Kent volunteered to be lowered aboard the back up boat. The pilot of the helicopter was rightfully reluctant. This would be a night lowering in very bad conditions: 14- to 16-foot seas, gusty winds 30- to 50-knots, in rain, snow, and hail. The official report of the incident says, "Petty Officer Kent convinced the pilot to attempt the hoist." The report says that the "hoist nearly failed when a huge wave popped up, but Petty Officer Kent adeptly touched and exited the sling in the nick of time." Kent then took

Master Chief Lars Kent, seated, and Chief Jon Gagnon comprised the top of the chain of command when author Dennis Noble visited Coast Guard Station Tillamook Bay, Oregon, for the purposes of researching this article. Since that time, Gagnon has moved on to Station Erie, Pennsylvania. Photo by Dennis Noble.

command of the motor lifeboat and prepared for the always difficult and dangerous night bar crossing. At just about this time, the Tillamook Bay area experienced a complete power outage due to winds gusting up to 113-knots. The outage darkened all the range and jetty lights, "leaving no visible reference to locate the bar area at night." The hovering helicopter provided "minimal lighting." As BM1 Kent approached the jetty, a heavy squall passed, lowering visibility to zero, and the motor lifeboat's radar failed. Kent turned the motor lifeboat into the seas to await the passing of the squall. Once passed, Kent again resumed his transit and brought the boat safely into the shelter of the bay.

Years later, Master Chief Kent would recall that after sorting everything out on the flare sighting case, "the reporting source figured out that she had been looking at the light on the entrance buoy." For his work on 14 and 16 December 1992, Lars Kent received his second Coast Guard Achievement Medal.[5]

Master Chief Kent said that the Tillamook Bay Station is the one unit he has most enjoyed during his career. He said the station has "one of the most challenging [operational areas], we have an incredible variety of … cases, from swimmers in distress, capsizings, stranded climbers on rocks, horses swept out to sea, and others." Although he enjoys his station, Master Chief Lars Kent plans on retiring at the end of his tour of duty.

The second in command at Tillamook Bay, Chief Boatswain's Mate (BMC) Jon W. Gagnon, was born on 28 January 1968. Like Master Chief Kent, Chief Gagnon listed Coeur D'Alene, Idaho, as home. Chief Gagnon has been married to Kim for 13 years and has two children.

Jon entered the U.S. Coast Guard on 7 July 1986 at the age of eighteen. He served aboard the buoy tender *Ironwood*, at Station Rio Vista, California, Aids to Navigation Team, Rio Vista, the 378-foot cutter *Midgett*, 378-foot cutter *Boutwell*, a first tour at Tillamook Bay, Station Coos Bay, Oregon, and in July 2000 reported to Tillamook Bay as the XPO.

Canadian Coast Guardsman Inga Thorsteinson inspects the lines of CG36513, *the 36-foot motor lifeboat now serving out its retirement from active service as a monument welcoming visitors to Coast Guard Station Tillamook Bay. Photo by John Galluzzo.*

Chief Gagnon said that Tillamook Bay is world-renowned for its fall salmon season, so September and October are the unit's busiest time. The crew is most apt to face the most dangerous cases, however, in the winter months. "The bar breaks on a regular basis and any rescue on the bar involves surf." A breaking bar is the one of the worst situations a mariner can encounter; breaking waves have more power than sea waves.

A U.S. Coast Guard captain once observed, "It is fun being the king. It is not always fun being the assistant to the king." Chief Gagnon, however, remarked that what he like most about being the XPO at Station Tillamook Bay is "being in a position to help and guide junior members of the command. I try to give them a straight path to follow." Jon pointed out that when a new person checks into the station, he also briefs them on "investments and the benefits of starting early." On the other hand, what Chief Gagnon does not like is "taking disciplinary action. If I have to take action I feel there was a failure in the system."

When asked how many people he estimated that he had saved, Chief Gagnon responded that if this meant actually reaching out and saving someone, "only one." But, if you mean taking action to prevent bad situations, "too many to count."

Chief Gagnon remembers a case while serving at Station Coos Bay on 25 October 1996. The tower watchstander tried, over the radio, to warn off the 60-foot fishing vessel *Chelsea* against crossing the bar. Despite the warnings, the captain of the *Chelsea* decided to try a crossing. The tower watchstander noticed the fishing vessel having difficulty in the heavy surf and called the station. The crews of the 44-foot motor lifeboat, *CG 44373*, and the 52-foot motor lifeboat *Intrepid* immediately got underway and crossed a bar with twelve foot breaking seas. At the same time, the station's beach rescue team made their way to the beach to help, if necessary. As the motor lifeboats arrived near the *Chelsea*, the fishing vessel, now disabled, drifted into 18-foot breaking seas. The seas pushed the *Chelsea* aground just off the beach. Two of the fishing vessel's crew abandoned their vessel. "Braving the cold water and dangerous surf, the beach rescue team recovered the two men and assisted them to shore." Breaking seas now exceeded twenty feet, but the two motor lifeboats continued to search for the missing crewman of the *Chelsea*. The two motor lifeboats remained outside the bar for five additional hours searching for the missing man, who later was found drowned.

Chief Gagnon remembered that "by the end of the night we were encountering 30-foot breaks." Chief Gagnon, as member of motor lifeboat *CG 44373*, along with the crews of the 52-foot motor lifeboat *Intrepid* and the station's beach rescue team, all received the U.S. Coast Guard Meritorious Team Commendation, with operational device.[6]

Shortly after helping me with this study, Chief Jon Gagnon received orders to be Officer-in-Charge of Station Erie, Pennsylvania. Chief Gagnon said that "Kim [Kimberly] and I are excited about our upcoming transfer to Erie. It will be a new part of the country for us and a larger city." On 14 June 2003, BMC Aaron Ferguson took over the duties of BMC Jon Gagnon.[7]

In April 2003, Station Tillamook Bay's crew size was officially set at forty-two. In addition to Officer-in-Charge and Executive Petty Officer, twelve crewmembers volunteered to fill out a questionnaire about themselves and their stations. What follows is not a "scientific survey," only a glimpse of the station.[8]

The average age of the people questioned was 28-years-old, with the youngest 21 and oldest 37 years old. The average age at the time of enlistment was 22.3 years old, with the youngest age 17 years old and the oldest 32 years old. One person had a GED (General Education Development), the rest had graduated high school and five had some college, with one person having four-years of college.

Why these people chose to enter the U.S. Coast Guard is interesting. Two came from families that had fathers who were career U.S. Coast Guardsmen. One of the two had a grandfather and father who served in the U.S. Coast Guard. One crewman said he enlisted "because I felt my calling after losing my brother … in a surfing accident." Another said he joined because he was "right out of high school with no job and I remembered watching the Coast Guard crews out on the boats when we would camp at Bodega Bay in California. I thought it would be interesting to do search and rescue." Another said that while he enlisted for all the things most recruiters stress: job security, training, good benefits, G.I. Bill, but "above all I felt that I owned my country for being there to protect me while I was young." The others gave reasons such as wanting to save people, help people, retirement system and money for school.

Only four of the twelve had not requested duty at the Tillamook Bay Station. Most wanted duty at the unit so they could work in the surf and

The Tillamook Bay Life-Saving Station at Barview is now a private residence. Photo by John Galluzzo.

perhaps gain the highest qualification of a small boat operator in the service, Surfman. Seven of the twelve were new to the service with Tillamook Bay Station being the first or second unit. One man had worked at six other units before reporting to the station.

Most of the people said what they liked about being stationed in Garibaldi, other than being able to work in the surf, was serving with their shipmates, the Master Chief and Chief. Interestingly, many enjoyed the community, "country living," "the beautiful Oregon coast," and one even liked the cool, rainy weather. Living in a rural area can be enjoyable, but, as some of the crew pointed out, what they did not like was lack of shopping, isolation, very few activities for a family and, a common complaint of anyone who has served as an enlisted person in the military, "low pay."

Only two of the twelve people who responded to the questionnaire said they did not know if they wanted to remain in the U.S. Coast Guard. This is an interesting response considering the question dealing with how many hours the crew felt they worked a week. The amount of hours

The Tillamook Bay Station sits among the natural beauty of the Oregon coastline. Photo by John Galluzzo.

per week ranged from 40-hours to a high of 112-hours. At another station, a crewman said a better question is: "How many hours a week do I not work?"

Ten of the twelve people were married and of these ten, seven had children. One crewman had five children.

One of the most interesting questions for a visitor to ask a crew: how many people have you personally saved? Anyone who has the opportunity to speak to a station crew should ask this question, the response to it says more than anything else about what the U.S. Coast Guard accomplishes in search and rescue. In this unscientific survey, the fourteen people examined estimated that they had personally saved thirty-eight people. As Chief Gagnon pointed out, however, the estimate does not count those warned from danger. One crewman, while as a crewman aboard a 378-foot cutter, reported that the cutter's crew rescued a boat load of hundreds of Haitians.

It has been my privilege over the last eight years to receive permission to visit with the people who serve at Station Tillamook Bay, Oregon. It is a long five-hour drive, one way, from my home to the unit.

I have never regretted the journey. The visits have allowed me to see the crew when they were "up" from a very good rescue and a few times when "down" from a bad case. The busy crew goes out of their way to make me feel welcome. At each visit, I learn something new, but also reconfirm some observations about stations that I have made since the first lifeboat station I went on board forty-six years ago. The young men and women of Station Tillamook Bay, along with their Officer-in-Charge and Executive Petty Officer, continue to try their best to serve those who work upon the waters of Oregon and the community they live within. They do this with very little notice from the people or country they serve. Perhaps this short examination shows that if you learn about station crews, you can also learn about exciting rescues.

About The Authors

Cara Blasko serves with the United States Coast Guard.

Margaret Thomas Buchholz is the Managing Editor of *The Beachcomber* (Ocean County, NJ), author of *Shore Chronicles, Diaries and Travelers' Tales from the Jersey Shore* and coauthor of *Great Storms of the Jersey Shore*.

Frederick G. "Bud" Cooney enlisted in the U.S. Coast Guard immediately after graduation from La Salle Academy in Providence, Rhode Island in 1951. He served on active duty as a seaman and later as a radioman. He entered the Coast Guard Reserve program and retired a Lieutenant Commander with thirty-eight years of combined service and is now fully retired with his wife Ann in Charlestown, Rhode Island.

CDR John F. Ebersole, USCG (Ret.) is the President of Excelsior College, the associate provost and dean, Extended Education, at Boston University. A retired commander with the U.S. Coast Guard, he held three commands, including a patrol boat in Vietnam, and was the recipient of two Bronze Stars and five Coast Guard and Navy commendations. He earned a Master of Public Administration and a Master of Business Administration from John F. Kennedy University, and is a distinguished graduate of the U.S. Naval War College. He holds a certificate of Management of Learning & Education from Harvard University and a Certificate in Pacific Basin Studies from the University of Southern California. During the fall of 2005, he held the Sandler Fellowship in Education at Harvard's Kennedy School of Government. In 2007, he completed an EdS degree from The George Washington University.

The late **Van R. Field** authored several important works on the maritime history of Long Island, New York, including *Shipwrecks and Rescues on Long Island*, *Mayday! Shipwrecks, Tragedies & Tales from Long Island's Eastern Shore*, and *New Jersey Shipwrecks and Rumrunners* (with John J. Galluzzo).

John J. Galluzzo is the editor of *Wreck & Rescue Journal*. Born in Hull, Massachusetts, the hometown of America's greatest life-saver, Joshua James, hc is a freelance writer contributing to newspapers and magazines throughout the South Shore of Boston area, with a focus on maritime history and modern day Coast Guard search and rescue stations. He has authored or coauthored thirty books on local history including *Lifesavers of the South Shore: A History of Rescue and Loss*, and penned the first chapter of the Foundation for Coast Guard History's book, *Coast Guard*.

David Gamage is a retired engineer residing in Maine. He's the grandson of a civilian light keeper and son of a Coast Guard Chief Boatswain's Mate whose career was search and rescue. As a freelance writer and researcher specializing in the history of Maine's lighthouses and life-saving stations, he has published several articles and contributed to works of other authors.

Eric C. Hartlep recently completed the manuscript for *Station 253: An Intimate History of the Middle Island Life-Savers, 1909 to 1920*. His interest in the USLSS, and Middle Island, Michigan, in particular, stems from the discovery that his great uncle, George A. Hartlep, was a surfman at Station 253 near Alpena, Michigan, during those years. George's 97-year-old daughter, Esther Hartlep Eddy, provided invaluable first-hand information that, together with station log reports from the National Archives, and period newspaper accounts, formed the basis for his work.

Nicholas Leach is an editor with *Ships Monthly* magazine and a well-known author on the history and the lifeboats of the Royal National Lifeboat Institution. His books include *The Lifeboat Service in Ireland, For Those in Peril: The Lifeboat Service of the United Kingdom and the Republic of Ireland Station by Station*, and *RNLI Motor Lifeboats: A Century of RNLI Motor Lifeboats*.

Carolyn Matthews was born in the Antipodes but has lived her adult life in Toronto. She has published the non-fiction *True Stories of Rescue and Survival: Canada's Unknown heroes*, *Heroic Rescues at Sea: True Stories of the Canadian Coast Guard*, *To the Rescue! True Stories of Tragedy and Survival*, award-winning short fiction, and feature articles in such newspapers as the *Toronto Globe and Mail* and the *National Post*.

Fred Miller, who lives in Ocean City, NJ, is a retired teacher and former Ocean City lifeguard, immediate past president of the Ocean City Historical Museum, director of the Ocean City Lifesaving Museum, member of the Ocean City Historic Preservation Commission, and a member of the Cape May County Culture and Heritage Commission. He and his wife, Susan, have written seven books on the history of Ocean City and surrounding areas: *Ocean City, America's Greatest Family Resort*; *Ocean City Beach Patrol*; *Ocean City 1950-1980*; *Ocean City Baby Parade*; *Ocean City, An Illustrated History*; *Atlantic City, An Illustrated History*; and *New Jersey's Southern Shore, An Illustrated History from Brigantine to Cape May Point*.

Dennis L. Noble is a retired Coast Guard senior chief with a doctorate in history from Purdue University. He is the author of eleven books on the history of the Coast Guard, including *That Others Might Live: The U.S. Life-Saving Service, 1878-1914*, *Lighthouses and Keepers: The U.S. Lighthouse Service and its Legacy* and *Lifeboat Sailors: Disasters, Rescues and the Perilous Future of the Coast Guard's Small Boat Stations*.

About The Authors

William D. Peterson is the author of *Images of America: United States Life-Saving Service in Michigan* and a museum professional currently living and working in Montana. A native of northern Michigan, he has spent much of his life in proximity to the old life-saving and lifeboat stations of the Great Lakes.

Geoffrey D. Reynolds has been the Director of the Joint Archives of Holland at Hope College since July 2001. Previous to that he served as the collections archivist since January 1997. He graduated from Wayne State University with a Masters in Library and Information Science (MLIS) and an Archival Administration Certificate in 1995. He currently serves as the treasurer of the Dutch-American Historical Commission, membership chairperson for the Association for the Advancement of Dutch American Studies, webmaster of the Michigan Oral History Association, Executive Director of the Holland Area Historical Society, newsletter and yearbook editor of the Water Wonderland Chapter of the Antique and Classic Boat Society, member of the History Advisory Council for Frederik Meijer Gardens and Sculpture Park, and board member of Holland, Michigan-based Michigan Shipwreck Research Associates. His research and writing interests include the pleasure boat building industry and restoring classic runabouts.

Frederick Stonehouse is the third president of the United States Life-Saving Service Heritage Association and received the 2006 award for Historic Interpretation from the Association for Great Lakes Maritime History. He is the author of numerous books on the maritime history of the Great Lakes, including *Wreck Ashore: The United States Life-Saving Service on the Great Lakes*, *The Wreck of the Edmund Fitzgerald*, and *Great Lakes Crime*. He has appeared nationally on the History Channel, Fox Family, and National Geographic.

Bob Trapani, Jr. is the Executive Director of the American Lighthouse Foundation, and the author of *Indian River Life-Saving Station: Journey Along the Sands*, *Delaware Lights: A History of Lighthouses in the First State*, *Lighthouses of Maryland and Virginia*, and *Lighthouses of New Jersey and Delaware: History, Mystery, Legends and Lore*.

Captain W. Russell Webster (USCG - Retired) is the former Group Woods Hole rescue commander and a veteran of 15,000 rescue cases. He is FEMA Region 1 (New England's) first-ever Federal Preparedness Coordinator, responsible for enhancing individual, community, state and federal preparedness for all hazards. "Coast Guard Tape of Harrowing 1980 Rescue Off Massachusetts Resurfaces" originally appeared in the July 4, 2004 edition of *The Cape Cod Times*.

END NOTES

The *Pendleton* Rescue

1. VAdm. Merlin O'Neill, USCG Commandant's remarks at Department of Treasury awards ceremony, 14 May 1952.

2. Information on the *Pendleton* is taken from U.S. Coast Guard Commandant Merchant Vessel Inspection Division, Marine Board of Investigation; structural failure of tanker *Pendleton* off Cape Cod on 18 February 1952, with loss of life, 25 September 1952. The Coast Guard's Board of Investigation concluded that low temperatures had tended to increase the notch sensitivity of the *Pendleton's* steel, resulting in brittle fractures. Excessive buoyancy in the bow and stern and heavy weight amidships created a sagging effect, which was aggravated by the extremely high seas.

3. Bernard C. Webber, Chatham, "The Lifeboat Men" (MA: Lower Cape Publishing, 1985), p. 43.

4. Capt. Charles B. Hathaway, USCG, (Ret.), "From Highland to Hammerhead, The Coast Guard and Cape Cod," Library of Congress card Number 00-130105, 2000, p. 133; and Commander Coast Guard District One, Boston, messages 182150z February 1952 and 191615z February 1952.

5. Webber, "The Lifeboat Men", p. 46.

6. Bernard D. Webber, correspondence with author, 27 September 2001.

7. Webber, "The Lifeboat Men", p. 46.

8. Webber, "The Lifeboat Men", p. 47.

9. Webber, letter to author, 27 September 2001.

10. Webber, letter to author, 27 September 2001.

11. Commander, Coast Guard District One, Boston. Record messages 181948z February 1952 and 191615z February 1952 indicated "near hurricane force winds" and that the much larger Coast Guard cutters *McCulloch* and *Legare* had suffered extensive weather damage during the rescue, including cracked plates and loss of life boats.

12. Webber, "The Lifeboat Men", pp. 47-48.

13. Webber, "The Lifeboat Men", pp. 47-48.

14. Webber, "The Lifeboat Men", pp. 47-48.

15. Webber, "The Lifeboat Men", pp. 47-48.

16. Webber, "The Lifeboat Men", pp. 47-48.

17. Hathaway, "From Highland to Hammerhead", p. 135.

18. Coast Guard Air Station Salem, MA, record message 182220z February 1952. The PBY thought the life boat was "experiencing radio troubles."

19. Webber, letter to author, 27 September 2001.

20. Commander, First Coast Guard District, Boston, record message 192129z February 1952.

21. In all, twenty-four Coast Guardsmen were honored for their efforts during the *Fort Mercer* and *Pendleton* rescues. Five Gold Lifesaving Medals, four Silver Lifesaving Medals, and 15 Coast Guard Commendation Ribbons were awarded to the rescuers.

Ships Fear Fire More Than Water

1. E.F. Babbage.

2. E.F. Babbage.

Lawrence O. Lawson: An Extraordinary Keeper

1. All material on Keeper Lawrence O. Lawson, unless otherwise noted, comes from photocopied material sent to Dennis L. Noble from the Evanston (IL) Historical Society.

2. U.S. Life-Saving Service Scrapbook, for year 1900, located in Record Group 26, Records of the U.S. Coast Guard, National Archives Building, Washington, D.C.

3. All material on the *Calumet* rescue, except the direct quotes from the Evanston Historical Society, are from the Historian of the U.S. Coast Guard's web site which lists the Gold Life Saving Medal recipients.

End Notes

Portrait of a Dying Breed: The Gilber's Bar House of Refuge

i Life-Saving Service Report 1882. Sumner Kimball.

ii York, Wick, Thesis.

2 Forty-third Congress, session I., chapter 344, June 20, 1874.

3 York, Wick. Thesis.

4 Hutchinson, Janet. "History of Martin County".

5 www.uscg.mil/hq/g-cp/history/stations/gilbertsbar.html

6 Hutchinson, Janet.

7 York, Wick, Thesis.

8 www.uscg.mil/hq/g-cp/history/stations/gilbertsbar.html

9 Hutchinson, Janet.

10 Report of the USLSS, 1878, Sumner Kimball.

xi Report of the USLSS, 183, Sumner Kimball.

xii The entire shipwreck section is taken from the USLSS Reports written annually by Sumner Kimball, Superintendent of the USLSS.

11 Shanks, Ralph and Wick York. "The U.S. Life-Saving Service". Pg 151.

xiii Hutchinson, Janet. Pg 59.

The Lifesavers of Coast Guard Station Tillamook Bay, Oregon

1. Unless otherwise noted, all quotations and personal information on crew are from a questionnaire prepared by the author in April 2003. The quote on size of the town was heard by the author during one of his visits to the station. So that I can respect the privacy of the crewmen completing the survey, I will not use names. Both Master Chief Kent and Chief Gagnon gave permission to use their names.

2. Information on station dates comes from, Dennis L. Noble, "A Legacy: The United States Coast Life-Saving Service" (Washington: Historian's Office, 1987), 26, and e-mail, BMCM Lars Kent and Dennis L. Noble,

3. E-mail, BMC Aaron S. Ferguson, XPO Station Tillamook Bay, to Dennis L. Noble, 26 April 2004.

4. Readers may recall the tragic accident of the charter fishing vessel *Tiki Tooo* on the Tillamook Bay bar on 14 June 2003. As there are still legal questions concerning this case, I will not discuss it in this article.

5. All material on the two cases comes from the citations and "Summary of Action" attached to Kent's questionnaire.

6. All material on rescue comes from citation attached to Gagnon's questionnaire.

7. E-mail, Ferguson to Noble, 26 April 2004.

8. I have heard crews from various stations say they receive too many official surveys to fill out, therefore I am pleased that some took the time from their schedules to complete an unofficial survey.

Association Information:

The United States Life-Saving Service Heritage Association

P.O. Box 213
Hull, Massachusetts 02045
www.uslife-savingservice.org
www.facebook.com/uslssh
www.twitter.com/uslssha